"This is a radical book, in the best possible senses of the word. It is radically biblical, in that the teaching is rooted in Scripture (unlike so many books on this subject that claim to be Christian and yet ape a secular worldview). It is radical in that it gets to the heart of a huge cultural shift going on right now in our society (it can be argued that the move from a Judeo-Christian outlook to a pagan outlook is best illustrated and epitomized in the change in the dominant view of gender issues in our culture). It is radical in that it gets down to the brass tacks of daily thinking, living and ministering (no head-in-the-clouds-ivory-tower stuff here!). Read it and put the truth to work. This truth frees."

J. Ligon Duncan III, Ph.D.
Senior Minister, First Presbyterian Church; Chairman, Council on Biblical Manhood and Womanhood; Adjunct Professor, Reformed Theological Seminary

"*Does Christianity Squash Women?* Rebecca Jones explores this penetrating question without resorting to platitudes or legalism, and she arrives at a triumphant answer. Her theological integrity makes this a challenging read. Her personal winsomeness makes it an enjoyable one. This book did for me what all good books do—it helped me to know Jesus better and love Him more. In this age of muddled messages regarding women and our roles, Christendom's message for women will resound more clearly as we join in Rebecca's courageous and gracious affirmation of biblical womanhood."

Susan Hunt
Presbyterian Church in America Women in the Church Consultant, Author, *The Legacy of Biblical Womanhood*

"Anybody studying or teaching about women in the Bible will find this book to be a storehouse full of treasures. Rebecca Jones combines sensitive, thoughtful interpretation of biblical narratives about women, rich theological insights about God's plan from Genesis to Revelation, and practical, real-life wisdom about the ways Christ meets the longings and deepest needs of women in contemporary culture. Jones does more than explain the Bible's teachings about the equality and differences between men and women—she clearly delights in those teachings, and, as a friend who has known her now for nearly forty years, I can attest that she faithfully lives out those teachings in her own life as well. It is a pleasure to recommend this excellent book!"

Wayne Grudem, Ph.D.
Research Professor of Bible and Theology
Phoenix Seminary, Phoenix, Arizona

"Merging societal norms and theological scholarship, Rebecca Jones challenges the readers of *Does Christianity Squash Women?* to candidly address the issues twenty-first-century women confront. The book's contents stimulate readers to honestly analyze women's concerns through the grid of Scripture and formulate conclusions that embrace a Christian worldview."

Pat Ennis
Professor and Establishing Chairperson, Department of Home Economics, The Master's College; Speaker, and Coauthor of *Becoming a Woman Who Pleases God* and *Designing a Lifestyle That Pleases God*

Does
CHRISTIANITY
SQUASH
Women?

Does
CHRISTIANITY
SQUASH
Women?

A CHRISTIAN LOOKS
AT WOMANHOOD

rebecca
JONES

BROADMAN
&HOLMAN
PUBLISHERS

13-digit ISBN: 978-0-8054-3091-2
10-digit ISBN: 0-8054-3091-1

Published by Broadman & Holman Publishers,
Nashville, Tennessee

Dewey Decimal Classification: 248.843
Subject Headings: WOMEN \ GOD \ CHRISTIANITY AND WOMEN

Unless otherwise noted, Scripture quotations have been taken from the Holman
Christian Standard Bible®, © 1999, 2000, 2002, 2003 by Holman Bible Publishers.
Other translations quoted are ESV, The Holy Bible, English Standard Version ©
2001 by Crossway Bibles, a division of Good News Publishers; NIV, © 1973, 1978,
1984 by International Bible Society; and KJV, public domain.

1 2 3 4 5 6 7 8 9 10 09 08 07 06 05

Dedication

I DEDICATE THIS BOOK TO MY FATHER, Edmund P. Clowney, who loved me unconditionally from the day I was born until the day he died, March 20, 2005. He was incurably generous, funny, tender, and encouraging. When I was a little girl, he washed my hair on Saturday nights, taught me to speak pig Latin, took me on Sunday afternoon walks, and told me scores of Bible stories. When I was older, he faithfully attended my field hockey games, came to my appearances in the latest school musicals, played chess with me, taught me to write poetry, munched ginger snaps with me on our mutual study breaks in the evenings, and showed me how to dream for the church. Throughout my life, his gentle compassion taught me of God's unfailing love.

Etched in my memory is a sun-drenched summer day in the beach town of Wildwood, New Jersey. I was only two at the time and lost on the boardwalk. Delivered to the boardwalk police by a solicitous older couple, I waited on a bench as I heard the announcement over the loudspeaker: "We have a little girl with brown hair and blue eyes, wearing a blue-and-white-striped sunsuit." As I waited, a tiny figure appeared in the distance, running toward me—my daddy! When he spotted me, he ran faster, arms outstretched to receive me. Soon I was safe and happy in his embrace. I would think of that image later when my dad preached about the prodigal son and the father who came running down the road to meet his lost boy.

My father often preached in northern New Jersey, taking one of his five children with him each time. When it was my turn, he would wake me early, make a hushed breakfast, and bundle me into the car for the two-hour drive, during which I would read the map for him and choose hymns for the service. In the sanctuary, I sat in the front pew, swinging my legs and listening to him preach Christ from the Old Testament. I would get goose bumps, even as an eight-year-old. I hardly knew why at the time. Now I know that my heavenly Father was teaching me through the mouth of my earthly father.

In March 2005, I had the glorious privilege and the unspeakable pain of sitting beside his bed for two weeks, as his life on earth drew to a close. Before medication and weakness deprived him of coherent conversation, I was able to tell him, much to his delight, that his latest book, which he had asked me to edit, had been accepted for publication (*How Jesus Transforms the Ten Commandments*). At 6:30 p.m. on Palm Sunday, we, his family, sang and prayed him into his heavenly Father's outstretched arms.

In addition to the huge sadness that threatened to overwhelm me after his death, a minor regret troubled me—that my father had not had time to put his editorial comments on the text of this book. But as I tearfully sorted through the writings and papers in his study, I found my manuscript with his encouraging editorial comments written on it! I present this book to you, dear reader, hopeful that it will encourage you to live as a godly Christian woman, just as my father's gracious words always encouraged me. In this small way, I can share him with you.

Contents

Preface

IN CONVERSATION WITH JAKKI, my hairdresser, I mentioned that I was writing a book. "Ah, yes," she said, when she heard the title. "But the question is, What's a woman?" I laughed and replied, "Exactly!" Then she asked me another pointed question: "Who's going to read your book?" My answer to her was, "I hope you will."

Well, here it is, Jakki, and I hope you will read it! I've tried to get rid of "jargon," but this is hard, for two reasons. First, I was raised with Christian vocabulary, so it's difficult to break the habit of familiar words. Second, some "jargon" words efficiently describe complicated ideas. When such terms are necessary, I'll explain them.

Jakki's question is a good one. Just what is a woman? Being a woman is not as easy as it might seem, and being a Christian woman is, in some ways, even more complicated. My five daughters have heard a cacophony of messages about what it means to be a woman. The society around them encourages them to be independent, to postpone marriage, to break the glass ceiling, to limit the number of children they have, and to make a real difference in the world. The Christian world has another set of confusing principles: Be in submission, set boundaries, concentrate on your marriage, find a career, enjoy your femininity, discover a new day for women in the church, keep silent in church, wear your hair long, and teach your children at home.

In this baffling context, young women panic. "Slow down!" they beg. "Let me sort it all out before I make my decisions." But time is a tyrant, demanding decisions. Your boss needs to know by tomorrow if you are going to accept the vice presidency of the bank or quit to stay home with your two-year-old. By Tuesday, you must decide whether or not to enroll in the premed course. Is becoming a doctor reasonable if you want to be married and have children? By next week, you have to let the school know if you will let your daughter join the coed wrestling team. Decisions, decisions. Should you keep living with your abusive husband? Should you push for more visibility in your church? Is it worth going to seminary if there are no job offers for women waiting for you when you graduate?

For wisdom, women do casual research by looking at other women—sisters, neighbors, friends, women in the media. Who is the happiest? What has worked for other women? But perhaps your sister, who counsels you about friendships, has no friends. Maybe your next-door neighbor leads a trouble-free life, but she spends her life at the mall or the health spa. Your neighbor has a great figure, swears by her weekly yoga class, travels to New York for her advertising firm, and has a darling three-year-old who is better behaved than the pastor's daughter. She even talks about God, but you're not sure it's the same God. Whose advice can you trust?

A Christian woman knows she cannot rely only on human advice. So she turns to the Bible to find her definition of womanhood. But the Bible describes all kinds of women: prostitutes, virgins, liars, warriors, lovers, mothers, nags, deceivers, gossips, prophetesses, independent business-women, widows, and martyrs. To our twenty-first-century minds, the Bible can seem antiwoman, yet it maintains that a woman is an equal shareholder in the kingdom of God, and "the glory of the man." It paints vivid pictures of seductive sexuality and stunning portraits of womanly strength, wisdom, and ingenuity. Can we see in the Bible a unified, over-arching definition of womanhood that brings together women from the Old and New Testaments and women living today?

It is humbling to tackle such a huge and controversial subject. I pray that God will make this book helpful to women who are thinking about how to live honestly with themselves as women. Some of you are asking how you can honor God in your female bodies and psyches. Others may still be asking Jakki's question: "What *is* a woman?" This book will examine God's definition of womanhood and challenge you to let God conform you to that definition. The Bible is one overarching mystery story, in which women play an essential role. God promised the first woman that one day a baby would be born who would provide a solution to the huge problem of death, sin, and suffering. The entire Old Testament has no meaning at all if it is not seen in relation to that promised baby.

But the promise is threatened with danger at every turn, because huge questions hang in the air of history: Will the promised baby arrive? Will the promised baby survive? It is as women are involved in this grand scheme of history that they find significance and joy. They are not bit players in this cosmic drama.

The identity, survival, and quest of this unique human being is the key to every woman's identity. It is this theme we will use to trace womanhood from the day the first woman was made right to the end of human history. We will start our story in the twenty-first century, however, asking whether women are still discontent after the feminist gains of the last generations. Then we will ask if there is anyone a woman can trust. In seeking to show what Christianity offers to the women's debate, we will examine God's contract with the universe and how it affects women. We will look briefly at *how* God tells us what we need to know, and we'll see how *not* to read the book that reveals our identity to us.

This foundation laid, we will plunge into the story of the mystery baby and examine women's role in bringing Him into the world. We will meet the odd women in Jesus' ancestry and examine how Jesus treats His physical mother and His spiritual mothers. Then we will look at the church, which still bears children for God, both in the physical and in the spiritual sense. Finally, in the context of the cosmic contract God made with His people, we will try to understand how twenty-first-century women can find satisfaction and meaning in their lives.

This book provides an overview. Other authors have written more detailed discussions of particular questions. I hope to clarify certain aspects of the women's debate by placing it in the context of the Bible's overarching story. Jesus taught that the whole Bible is about Him. If this is true, then we can only understand what it teaches us about women if we keep the debate focused on Jesus. Some of this book may seem somewhat abstract or theological for that reason, but I would not be faithful to Jesus if I spoke of experience alone. We go hopelessly astray if we try to understand women without respecting the underlying principles of the Bible's story.

Being a woman may seem complicated, but it is also simple. Being a real woman is believing and acting on the truth that we have been set apart for a special job by Jesus Christ our Creator and Savior, who was Himself born of a woman. Ultimately, Jakki, only God can answer your question: "What's a woman?" When we accept God's authority to define and use us, we discover what it means to be a woman.

Using this Book

I have included questions and resources for each chapter in the book. The questions are the kind I like: no fill-in-the blanks! They will stimulate you to think and to dig into your Bibles. There are few "right" answers. For group Bible study, the leader and group members should feel comfortable with open-ended questions. If you get stuck after studying the Scripture, ask the best Bible scholars in your congregation for help.

I trust you will find the resources list helpful. If you wish to interact with me, feel free to e-mail me through our Web site: www.cwipp.org.

*I'm the anorexic girl . . . . It's my identity. . . . My nickname is Itty-Bitty,
so what am I going to be without it? It's what makes me special.*
—ERIN, 24

Girls rule better. I love girls. They rock. And they rule. And boys drool.
—LILY, 6

1

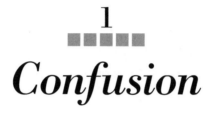

Confusion

ONE DAY MY FOURTEEN-YEAR-OLD daughter brought home a lesbian friend. During their evening of conversation, my daughter asked her if she liked guys. "Oh sure," she replied.

"Which do you like better?" my daughter asked. "Girls or guys?"

"I guess I like guys better," answered her friend.

With inscrutable teenage wisdom, my daughter replied, "Why don't you just do nothing, then, until you figure it out?"

This confusion is no longer unique to the teens of California. It's exotic to be a lesbian, or at least a "bi." Older women, though perhaps less accepting of lesbianism, grapple with the age-old problems of attracting, dominating, competing with, ignoring, needing, despising, and emasculating men (sometimes more than metaphorically). Some argue that the reigning sexual confusion is good because the pieces now spinning in the air will fall down into a better pattern for society.[1]

What Has Feminism Accomplished?

What about it? Are we better off for the open-mindedness about sexuality which was introduced, in large part, by the feminist movement over the last generation? Feminism has changed since the 1970s when I was a student at a women's college. Today there is ecofeminism, anarchist feminism, liberal feminism, legal feminism, global feminism, independent feminism, third-wave feminism, multicultural feminism, pro-life feminism, evangelical feminism . . . and the list goes on. Feminism has fallen prey to its own success. It so successfully challenged our instinctive answer to the question, what's a woman? that it decimated our definitions of sexuality. If we don't know what a woman is, defending her rights becomes dicey. Take this oddity, for example: "Smith College—the historic women's institution—has amended its student constitution to exclude the pronouns 'she' and 'her'. Why? As a news story explained, 'a growing number of students identify themselves as transgender, and say they feel uncomfortable with female pronouns.'"[2]

Not only have we lost the male representative pronoun, but we must eliminate "she" because some women don't define themselves as women! The pressure on language is so great that one Christian student leader wrote me an e-mail referring to a female student as "they." She might have chosen the alternative pronouns proposed by some: "ze" instead of "he" or "she" and "hir" instead of "him" or "her."[3] Feminism is a dragon devouring its own tail. It is so divided that it can no longer defend women because it can't define them.

One feminist was shocked to realize that she was shocked that *women* had participated in the abuse of Iraqi prisoners: "As a feminist who has always supported equality for women in the military, I am so disturbed by the role of women in these atrocities that I have difficulty explaining the intensity of my reaction."[4] Somewhere down deep, this feminist is expecting women to act as . . . well, women!

Some feminists have tried to find a definition agreeable to most women. Here is one such attempt: "Liberal feminism does not deny differences, but assumes that *whatever they may be,* they do not justify denying women their rights as human beings, or circumscribing their rights as social and legal subjects, *whatever these rights may be*"[5] (emphasis mine).

This woman affirms differences she can't discern and claims rights she can't define. This sounds like an expression we learned in France: *Je ne suis ni pour ni contre, bien au contraire!* ("I'm neither for nor against—on the contrary!")

Other feminists claim to know exactly what "these rights may be." They forge ahead with radically independent movements, calling for individual liberty at all costs and sanctioning any and all sexual expressions, whether lesbianism, pornography, prostitution, pedophilia, or bestiality. While such "anything goes" feminism would, for example, support the "rights" of children to have sex with whomever they wish at whatever age, other feminists feel called to protect children (as soon as they are born, at any rate).

Radical feminist thinkers are everywhere in academia, not only in the women's studies departments. We women need to know what is being proposed in our name. The University of Wisconsin's health department, for example, sponsored talks by Susie Bright, author of a book called *Sexual State of the Union.* The university Web site describes Bright as a "national 'sexpert' . . . [who] talks candidly about sex and sexuality. She edits the popular 'Best American Erotica' series; has written for *Salon, Playboy,* and *Penthouse*; and conducts workshops on erotic writing . . . . Her talk is presented by Sex Out Loud, a UW-Madison project for sexual health. The event is sponsored in part by the University Health Services."[6]

Some feminists dissociate themselves from the Susie Brights of the women's movement. They limit themselves to achieving political gains for women in the workplace or to promoting economic independence for women in countries where education for women is restricted. Because they define feminism so broadly and practically, these activists are distressed that most women do not think of themselves as feminists. It appears that the average woman considers feminism to be of the radical, not the practical, bent and, when interviewed, immediately protests that she is not a "man-hater." Although she is in favor of women's social rights, she is reluctant to support feminism even by the simple act of voting for another woman at the polls.

However fractured the feminist movement may be, it has created in our society certain expectations. Women expect equal pay for equal work. They expect to be heard and respected. They expect to participate fully in academics, sports, politics, the work world, the armed services, and the church. They expect to make their own decisions about their bodies and their health. If they have children, they expect men to share in rearing them. They consider contraception normal, and barrenness a choice rather than a stigma. This practical feminism means women run their own lives without barriers caused by gender. We have realized Kate Millett's dream, expressed in 1970: "Women's autonomy is what women's liberation is all about."[7]

Global Womanhood

Defined in this loose way, practical feminism has gone global. The Internet, global commerce, global law, and global democracy are new to our generation, making practically all issues global. As democracy spreads, women's rights are a part of the package. The United Nations and its cooperating agencies have produced documents approved by scores of nations that define women's rights to mean, among other things, her right to reproductive self-rule.[8] The nongovernmental organizations implementing such programs offer much help to Third World women: good health care, schools for girls, information about HIV-AIDS, and loans allowing them financial independence.

Part of the moral imperative of such UN-style democracy is to arrive at the level of physical comfort and wealth necessary to assure the happiness of women, families, and nations—and even the earth itself.[9] To achieve this utopia, the human family must learn to limit its consumption and conserve its natural resources. In addition, it must not have more children than it can afford. In this new economic equation, our reproduction must not outstrip our gross national product.

In the context of such global morality, abortion-rights advocates become saviors of the globe, guaranteeing women their freedom and the earth a sustainable environment for the happy life of future generations. Extrapolations of birth rates have caused us to imagine catastrophic overcrowding. To achieve a balanced, sustainable, global human family, contraception and abortion have been added to the key pillars of education, economic stability, and democracy. So contraception and sterilization are offered to help women reduce their country's reproduction rate to the desired "below replacement" level, which is under an average of about 2.1 children per couple.

Part of the laudable attempts to bring wealth and education to Third World countries is the questionable assumption that women will make "better" choices about fertility. Ironically, many Third World women, when asked what they would do differently if they were better off financially, responded, "I'd have more children"![10]

Lending money to a woman for a sewing machine will have a short-term beneficial effect of keeping her present family alive. Worthy goals such as protecting young girls from abuse and forced prostitution, educating women, fighting famine and poverty, and banning cultural practices such as clitoridectomy and wife-burning are sometimes most passionately promoted by those whose goal it is to tear down "patriarchal" despotism and drastically to reduce the world's population.[11]

Will our world be happier with fewer people in it? Or do ecofeminists actually throw the warm bathwater out with the babies?

The Fruits of Independence

How do women fare under feminist cultural rules? Ironically, the emphasis on independence has left many women twisting in the wind. A friend of mine moved to the United States from Singapore, where women's roles were much more tightly defined. Oddly enough, she was shocked to see how little respect American women commanded. Having severed their dependence on men and the family structure, women are forced to prove that they can make it on their own. Independence has come at a great price.

Women have the freedom to earn the same salary as a man, but he may no longer earn enough to support a wife and children, which obliges his wife to work, even if she would prefer to stay home. How drastically has the influx of women into the marketplace cut available jobs for men? Women who used to have the leisure to read to their children or to serve in the local soup kitchen with their church are now under the yoke of a boss who often runs not only their work life but, by default, their family lives as well.

We all know that children are growing up rootless, dependent on the babysitting services of day care centers, the television, the computer, the Xbox, or even the local gang. They lack a secure foundation for maturity and for developing healthy relationships. Women who have listened to the whispers of society that their lives are worth nothing unless they have a job and a career outside the home must now watch in anguish as their children are being murdered by or (worse yet) are murdering their classmates. Women's bid for autonomy has made their children autonomous by default. Such little ones, without the presence of a strong yet merciful mother, are growing up rootless, without morality. Meanwhile, women are pouring their best into the corporation, instead of into their children, whom they love so dearly.[12]

Women do not want to be careless mothers. In their attempt to be true to themselves and to their sex, women have relied on their fortitude, courage, fidelity, and hardworking natures to go on overload. Many forego sleep to "do it all." My college five- and ten-year class notebooks were full of stories of successful women living on four hours sleep each night. Many women work harder than their male counterparts so that the name of women will be respected. The hardworking professional woman does not wish to forego motherhood, so she cuts back on work in the middle of her career to make time for a baby or two. Because men generally do not participate equally in home chores, women often work ninety-hour weeks, trying to succeed on all fronts.

Not only have women foregone the luxury of staying at home; they have taken on the entire responsibility of protecting themselves. Feminism's assumption that a woman's body belongs to her alone has left her vulnerable physically. Men are happy to agree that the woman's body and whatever life has begun to grow within it are the sole responsibility of the woman. "If you're in charge of your body, then you deal with the baby!" Many teenage girls are faced with three equally distasteful options: accept an unwanted abortion, live the grueling life of a single mother, or marry a selfish lout. She goes for her abortion alone, bears her baby alone, or holds the couple together in the even more crushing loneliness of a loveless marriage.

For thirty years, feminism has been repeating the mantra, "I can look after myself, thank you!" On an e-mail newsletter for a cancer group, I was shocked to read of a man who divorced his wife when he found out how much care her multiple myeloma would demand from him. But the woman who thinks of herself as the sole owner of her body should *expect* the man to walk away when that body no longer pleases him. Why shouldn't he? It's her body, after all!

Like men, women have insisted that sex be detached from commitment and from procreation. The loose view of marriage vows has freed her from commitment; contraception and abortion have freed her from children. But the satisfaction is empty, because even Susie Bright regrets having given in on a whim to the sexual advances of her auto mechanic.[13] Droves of thirty-five-year-old women, startled by the loud alarm bell of their biological clocks, are consulting fertility experts in a frantic urge for children. The intimacy of physical sex without commitment and love is, perhaps especially for women, an agonizing deception.

Women's Guilt

Women have staggered through the feminist upheaval under a load of guilt: I should have been a better wife. I could have been the manager if only I'd worked harder. I never knew how to be a good mother. I should never have had an abortion. I should have had children sooner. If only I had gotten my doctorate. Maybe I'm too tied to money. Maybe I'm not asserting myself enough. What did I do wrong that no one wants to marry me?

Women do not easily rid themselves of a sense of duty. Somewhere, deep in their womanly souls, no matter how loudly they have proclaimed their feminist rights, there is a gnawing sense that they should *be* or *do* things they have never managed to be or do. Here are several areas that seem to plague us.

Have We Made Men into Wimps?

Women are forever unhappy with men. Feminists decry patriarchy and hate men for dominating. Christian women complain because their husbands are not leaders. Single women feel offended if a man opens a door for them. By the time she is thirty, a woman is disgusted that the men her age want younger women, who will bend to their desires. Where is the mature young man who respects a woman, yet knows what he wants and says so?

Feminism has certainly achieved the destruction of all our social rules. A girl used to know the romantic stages. If a man asked her out to a movie, he was interested. In my high school days, there was the "going steady" stage, and then an official engagement, leading to marriage. I am not glorifying the particular social code under which I grew up, but most cultures have some kind of accepted set of steps leading to marriage. Today, the societal signals are totally confused.

Feminism has discouraged and frightened young men. If they declare themselves, they are macho and old-fashioned. To pay for dinner has become an insult. If they hang back, they are wimps. "Why doesn't he at least invite me out!" In giving the woman total independence, feminism may have comforted men in their natural laziness while confounding any desire for responsibility. A selfish, postfeminist man walks in and out of a woman's life even more easily than the scoundrels of earlier eras. Women hardly know at whose feet to lay the blame. Even as they spit vitriol at men, they are uneasy, wondering how they could/ should have behaved differently.

Have We Denied Motherhood?

Under their bravado, women wonder if they have made the right choices. The longer they have lived with those choices, the harder it is to admit that they may not have been wise. Some women approaching their forties suddenly wake up with an overwhelming desire for children. They regret the years "lost" to work, especially when their bodies will not cooperate with their desire to bear a child. This desire is so strong that women often sidestep marriage to have children. Hence we see singles and lesbians adopting children or seeking artificial insemination. Their married counterparts drop out of work, spending their forty hours a week seeking fertility treatment instead of looking for a promotion or a higher salary. In desperation, some have turned to surrogate mothers and even cloning.

Have Desires Destroyed Deep Joy?

As women age, they realize that desires and joy are not the same thing. They have received recognition in the academic world, or a six-figure salary, but they are no closer to deep joy. One extremely successful graduate of a well-known women's college wrote a fascinating article in her alumnae magazine. After her second marriage succumbed to the pressure of two separate careers, she concluded that her first husband had been right: "It takes two people to make one success." What an astounding admission from a woman who had tried so hard to meet the expectations of the feminist agenda.

Career women may later regret what their more traditional counterparts have—children and grandchildren for whom to buy gifts at Christmas, and a son or daughter to take them to the doctor when they are sick. The "family" woman visits her grandchildren or sits in her own cozy home, comfortable with a man whose very breathing patterns she can predict instinctively. Bitter disappointment can creep over the lonely career woman, but there is no market where she can exchange three lovers and a Ph.D. for a grandchild.

Career is one temptation. Absolute sexual freedom is another. Exercising the sexual autonomy handed to women by feminism has left some with a legacy of physical disease or a sense of worthlessness. Feminism voiced a double message: Don't depend on feminine wiles for your value, but use them when and as you wish. Our attitude toward our sexuality is convoluted and full of stress. Feminism has fought to free young women from an unhealthy dependence on physical beauty, but it can never erase the natural "sexiness" of girls.

Lauren Greenfield, a poignant photographer of the tensions and motivations of girls, has produced a powerful essay called "Girl Culture," in which she explores the attitudes girls have about their own bodies. In her essay we find this astounding comment from six-year-old

Lily: "Girls rule better. I love girls. They rock. And they rule. And boys drool."[14] Women have always had and will always have a "power vs. subjection" battle about their sexuality and their bodies. They hate what they think places them in an inferior position of dependence on men, while at the same time reveling in the power over men that sexuality gives them. As Lauren Greenfield's study shows, the average American young woman lives in a culture very different than the one in which her counterpart lived one hundred years ago. As Joan Jacobs Brumberg put it, "On the basis of my reading over one hundred personal diaries written by adolescent girls between 1830 and 1980, I concluded that as the twentieth century progressed, more and more young women grew up believing that 'good looks'—rather than 'good works'—were the highest form of female perfection."[15]

Autonomy makes the tension worse, of course. A woman in a loving relationship with a man finds no difficulty in emphasizing both good looks and good works.

Is Abortion on Our Conscience?

Those who have paid for their freedom with the lives of their own children are especially prone to excruciating disappointment and guilt. The shadows of an abortion dissipate slowly, even for a woman who has sought and found forgiveness from God. For the woman who cannot bring herself to define an abortion as the destruction of her child, the guilt seeps down into all her attitudes, producing unnamed sources of bitterness, anger, irritability, and depression. She faces not only what she has done, but the destruction of the dreams that could have been. The tiniest child who lives in the womb of his mother leaves his fingerprints on her soul. She remains his mother, whether he lives or dies. The pall of abortion guilt chokes our generation of women like a spiritual smog and weighs on our collective female conscience.

Does Our Virginity Matter?

Guilt comes also when a woman gives her body over and over again to various clients, whether to high school friends, a series of husbands, or hundreds of clients. The argument that a woman owns her own body has, ironically, fostered sexual profligacy, encouraging a woman to give her body to men who have no respect for it! The "sex-positive" feminists may mock the advocates of abstinence, but they have a hard time convincing us that they show ownership of their bodies by giving sex to the auto mechanic.

What joy is there in controlling one's body if it has been possessed and discarded by a countless series of selfish men? Surely a woman declares her ownership of her body more powerfully by keeping her sexual attention for a man who truly loves her, who will cherish that body as much as she does. Is the abstinent teen really the dupe of the religious right? Is she not rather the one who is truly free to give her body, since no one else has yet taken it? Sexual intimacy is so powerful that when women use it lightly, they plunge into a valley of shadow. Those shadows thicken, and women cannot escape, because the bodies they own, in which they sleep, eat, and live, are the very ones they have sullied.

One way to ignore such guilt is to divide the body and the soul. The body can do what it wants and the soul remains detached. It is perhaps in this way that women can become prostitutes and still have some sense of personal value. Far from owning their bodies, they have abandoned them to another world, where they float, detached from mind and soul.

Women's Spirituality: Finding the Center

To resolve the guilt in which they live, women have sought inner peace. They look to yoga, exercise, diet, and alternate spiritualities. Some women have split their bodies from their souls by allowing themselves to be caught up in loveless sex or abortions. They seek to bring the two entities together in "new" forms of spirituality that are no longer defined by organized religion and accepted moral codes, but by acts of individual or group reflection, meditation, and prayer.

The RE-imagining conferences were sponsored by women in the Presbyterian Church USA to promote a progoddess, antipatriarchal kind of spirituality. After these notorious conferences died out, small groups of women have continued to meet locally to explore their feminine spirituality. One group described their "RE-imagining" meeting this way: "We painted our fingernails bright purple, put on tattoos, blew bubbles, ate M&M's (plain and peanut) and on and on. It was a great way to affirm the freedom we felt as women in our lives together."[16] What leads women to such silly and embarrassing behavior as they search for their spiritual and feminine identity?

The world toppled statues of Marx and Lenin because it realized that flat, atheistic materialism could not feed the soul. Humans need "soul food," and our society offers chicken soup and other hearty dishes for the soul. We have become spiritually sensitive and are openly exploring the world of the spirit. In my local paper, an article informed me that a ghost-busting team had been hired, using tax money, to clean one Washington building of spirits, since so many people were convinced it was haunted. Evidence of our openness to such spirituality is everywhere—from the bookstore to the health spa, from the Presbyterian Church to the local writer's group.

In our new push for spirituality, women are favored conduits to wisdom. The intuitive powers of women make them excellent ghost busters, mediums, and spiritual guides. They are in tune with their emotions, with the throbbing center of the earth and with the spirits who presumably run it. Modern women rediscover spirituality by finding the "center" of their feminine selves.

Even Christian women practice "centering prayer," looking for a world between the worlds, where they are at peace. The bustle of work and family life and the tensions of crime, war, and economic uncertainty have left women overworked and tense. In that magic center, they seek a source of happiness, peace, and direction, which they can then offer to their families, communities, pets, and environment. In that guilt-free place, we can bring our bodies and souls back together, discovering the "balance" of our dark and light sides, of our male and female elements.

In downtown Manhattan, a gathering of sophisticated editors of mass-market women's magazines met to discuss trends in marketing to the twenty-first-century woman. A summary of their meeting states: "What all these publications aim to do . . . is to tap into a spirit stirring the new millennium—a trend more spiritual, a fascination with the interior lives of real people, and a hunger for more substance in daily living."[17] Have today's "spiritual" women found what they are seeking?

What do women really want?

What Women Want

I have had a particularly intense relationship with the middle of my five daughters. Though not lacking in passion, I am too "cut and dried" for my volatile daughter. While I doggedly insist on logic, common sense, and consequences, she drinks in the pleasurable imaginations of a thousand possibilities, intoxicated with the very confusion. She knew exactly how to exasperate me. When she was a child, she would come into the kitchen while I was cooking dinner for our family of nine and lay her math text in the middle of the food-covered counter.

"Mom, can you help me for a minute?"

"After dinner, sweetheart."

"But I have so much homework!"

"You should have started earlier."

"I was practicing piano."

"Is it a quick question?"

"Oh, yes."

I peer at the book, greasy fingers hovering in the air, and ask, "What's the assignment?"

"I'm not sure."

"I think you have to find the diameter of the circle."

"No, I don't think so."

"You said you didn't know what the assignment was, so I'm looking at the sample problems."

"The teacher said we weren't supposed to do it like that."

"Well how did the teacher explain it, then?"

"I don't know. That's why I'm asking you."

"I can't read your teacher's mind and I have to finish dinner. If you know what to do, then go back to your room and do it."

"See, you never want to help me with my homework!"

We women are like that unreasonable child. We're not sure what we want, except to know that the one thing we *don't* want is what's on offer. Deep in nearly every woman's soul is a desire for the following:

- Good, intimate relationships with the men and women in our lives. Tender fathers, caring brothers, a loving husband, trust-worthy women friends and mentors. Solid relationships based on honesty, commitment, and affection.
- Children.
- A place to call home—not only walls and rooms but a safe "sit by the fire" place where we can be ourselves without fear and where others can receive something from us.
- Significance. Doing something that really counts in the world, something only we can offer.

Because these desires seem mutually exclusive, women tend to give up hope in one realm to find satisfaction in another. The career woman decides it's not realistic to have children. The stay-at-home mom de-cides she can't bother with the outside world. The abused woman gives up on meaningful relationships with men. The sex kitten signs away her expectations for true friendship with other women. The divorcee resigns herself to living out of a camping van.

Is it possible to "have it all"? This is a question Danielle Crittenden raises in *What Our Mothers Didn't Tell Us*. She was surprised to discover that thirty years of feminism have left women still unhappy. "Women today enjoy unprecedented freedom and opportunity," she states.

So why, I'd wondered, were the articles in women's magazines so relentlessly pessimistic? I'd pulled thirty years' worth
of back issues of *Mademoiselle, Glamour, Vogue, Redbook,
Cosmopolitan,* and *McCall's* from the stacks of the Library
of Congress. It was partly from reading magazines like these
that Betty Freidan had concluded in 1963 that the women of
her generation felt unhappy and stifled. A huge social transformation had taken place. . . . Had it made women any happier? . . . From . . . a general gauge of mood, . . . the answer
was, resoundingly, no.[18]

Crittenden suggests that it is time to reevaluate. She advocates bear-
ing children early and developing a career once they are in school. She counsels today's young woman not to delay marriage too long, and to be more sensible about how many suitors she turns down, waiting for Mr. Perfect. However, Crittenden's suggestions do not get to the heart of the problem. She does not ask the important question that Jakki asked me: What is a woman? Who defines womanhood? How we answer this question will determine our goals, our actions, and our satisfaction.

On this level, the feminist issue brings us to the heart of what can only be a religious question. Feminism began by attacking societal structures that support male authority. Take, for example, the statement by Virginia Mollenkott, until recently identified by Christians as an evangelical: "Patriarchy is a profoundly mistaken social system that has caused misery to millions and could yet cause the destruction of humankind and the planet we share together."[19] Andrew Greeley says, "Today we are experiencing the last gasp of a dying order, and in twenty years most of it will be gone. . . . Women will remake religion."[20] (The twenty years are up and they have!)

Ultimately, such feminism must shake its fist not only at human patriarchs, but at the Judeo-Christian God. Naomi Goldenberg understood the radical nature of the conflict: "The feminist movement in Western culture is engaged in the slow execution of Christ and Jahweh. Yet very few of the women and men now working for sexual equality within Christianity and Judaism realize the extent of their heresy."[21] Thinking that freedom must end in a *coup d'état,* we women have stormed the very throne room of the ultimate patriarch, God.

Only Christianity offers true satisfaction to women. As in all areas, it gives us "more than we could ask or think." Only a Christian woman can begin to understand who she needs to be. The Christian faith satisfies a woman's needs in all the above-mentioned areas. It offers her a loving, faithful Father, sound and satisfying friendships with men and with other women. It gives her the wisdom and power necessary to control her body, to enjoy her sexuality, and to bear and rear children. It gives her a place to call home and allows her to have an influence not only in her family and community but on the future of the world.

Danielle Crittenden never mentions the one most important thing our mothers forgot to tell us: Only God can reveal what it means to be a woman.

■ ■ ■

Discussion Questions

1. How do you define "feminism"?

2. Think of three women you know well. What are their main fears? Their disappointments? Their hopes?

3. Do you feel betrayed in any way as a woman? If so, how?

4. Have you tried something new recently in order to enhance your spiritual life? If so, what? Has it worked?

5. Do you resist the idea that God has the right to define you as a woman?

6. How do your fears and disappointments differ from those of your mother's generation? Of your daughter's generation (or today's young girls)?

7. Do you find men too wimpy or too macho? Give some examples from your own life.

8. What's your impression of the place of women in Christianity? What experiences have you had with Christian women? Are they good or bad?

9. What differences are there between men and women? How do you define femininity?

10. Do you think feminism and Christianity are compatible or incompatible? Explain your thinking.

■ ■ ■

Resources

Crittenden, Danielle. *What Our Mothers Didn't Tell Us: Why Happiness Eludes the Modern Woman.* New York: Simon and Schuster, 1999.

Davis, Philip G. *Goddess Unmasked: The Rise of Neo-pagan Feminist Spirituality.* Dallas: Spence Pub., 1999.

Gabler, Neal. *Life: The Movie.* New York: Random House Vintage, 2000.

Jones, Peter. *Spirit Wars: Pagan Revival in Christian America.* Mukilteo, Wash.: Winepress Publishing, 1997.

Hensley, Jeff Lane, ed. *The Zero People*. Ann Arbor, Mich.: Servant Books, 1983.

Kassian, Mary. *The Feminist Gospel: The Movement to Unite Feminism with the Church*. Wheaton, Ill.: Crossway, 1992.

Moore, Terrence O. "Wimps and Barbarians: The Sons of Murphy Brown," www.claremont.org/writings/crb/winter2003/moore .html.

Sproul, R. C. *Abortion: A Rational Look at an Emotional Issue*. Colorado Springs, Colo.: NavPress, 1990.

Wells, David. *God in the Wasteland: The Reality of Truth in a World of Fading Dreams*. Chicago: Eerdmans, 1994.

www.missionamerica.com

www.greenfield.viiphoto.com/girlculture/index.html

Will I ever trust men again?
My husband made sweet love to me last week. This week he told me
he's in love with someone else and wants a divorce.

2
■ ■ ■ ■ ■

Trust

WHEN I WAS SPEAKING IN Geelong, Australia, I met a thirty-eight-year-old TV screenwriter. Elegant, creative, and intelligent, this young woman told me that neither she nor any of her six female friends from university days were now married or have children. One friend had gone through three husbands. The others had been deserted by their partners. No one had warned them that their well-laid plans for career and family would disintegrate when the men walked out.

Can we still trust? To understand how women can be happy and satisfied, we must get to the root of the trust issue. Is there any reliable foundation on which we can build our lives?

Commitment + Trust

Women can have satisfying relationships and discover worth both within and outside the family. They can create a true home and bear children to men who are faithful to them.[1] A happy woman, like a happy man, is a woman whose relationships are grounded in commitment and trust. Here is where one of those jargon words comes in handy. I shall call a relationship based on trust and commitment a "covenant" relationship. Though little used, the term *covenant* still refers to a solemn commitment between two parties. The Treaty of Versailles contained the Covenant of the League of Nations. A wiccan cooperative belongs to "the Covenant of the Three Wells." I live near San Diego, California, where there is an extremely fancy neighborhood nicknamed "the Covenant" because homeowners must sign a binding contract to a homeowners' association.

In a covenant, each party agrees to fulfill certain responsibilities. Rewards result if the covenant is kept, and consequences occur if it is broken. We enter into covenants constantly. We sign credit card agreements, mortgages, software licenses, educational loans, and our tax returns. Our signature signifies that we will abide by certain rules and that we understand the consequences for breaking them. Though we regret certain agreements, we are often glad that our signature guarantees us protection. I remember my relief when, on reading the fine print in my credit card agreement, I discovered that my insurance *did* pay for the side view mirror I knocked off a rental car while driving through Liverpool, England.

Such promises not only protect us in our relationship with the state, our boss, or our neighbors; they also control that central human relationship—marriage—which, above all others, is based on mutual trust and commitment.

The Nature of Covenant Promises

Sure

We prize those people in our lives who have kept their promises. But fulfilled promises depend on two things: honesty and commitment. We value friends who are honest about themselves, about life, and even about us. But honesty is not the only necessary factor in dependability. For a covenant arrangement to take place, *commitment* must be joined to trustworthiness: "I will be faithful to you until death." A man's trustworthiness is useless to a woman until he commits it to her personally in a lasting promise. And his promise is worthless unless it is backed by a trustworthy character.

Two human beings cannot promise such fidelity to each other without accepting the notion of sacrifice: I will put your needs above my own. Or, as my college motto goes, *non ministrari sed ministrare,* "not to be ministered unto, but to minister" (Matt. 20:28 KJV). I used to tell my children that the only argument I wanted in our home was: "You go first!" "No, you go first!" (unless they were arguing about cleaning the kitchen).

Personal

Promises engage us personally. They assume that we are other than rocks and trees. There is a "face-to-face" notion about vows that recognizes the value of each individual and an equally important value to the unit created by the joining of those two individuals. The first man's reaction to the first woman was the Hebrew equivalent of a "Wow!" followed by the "in-your-face" nature of the relationship: "Wow! Surely *this* is flesh of my flesh and bone of my bones," says Adam, when he wakes to find that his dream is not a dream. Before him stands a breathtakingly beautiful companion, truly worthy of him. The marriage covenant is unique among human promises, because it is a lifelong commitment and because it is the most intimate of relationships, an owning of another person's body.

Whole

The promises made in a covenant marriage structure are such that both body and soul are engaged. True marital fidelity keeps body and soul together, avoiding the two extremes created by a split between the physical and the spiritual: debauchery (since the body is considered of no importance) or self-denial (since the body and its desires are to be suppressed). True covenant relationship between a man and his wife allows a man to see his wife's physical beauty and rejoice, while also loving her whole person. It allows a woman to absorb the physical attention of her husband without refusing the soul attachment that is linked to it. Spirituality and physicality join for true communion. My husband and I (who still have a lot to learn about marriage) have hit on a formula for Christian marital success: "A woman must realize that it is godly to be sexy, and a man must realize that it is sexy to be godly."

Intimate

Trust allows honesty. Honesty within a couple means that love continues in spite of weak or willfully selfish behavior. The grace necessary in such relationships engenders tenderness and forgiveness which, when received, creates a desire to render in kind. When a woman senses that her man knows everything about her and loves her still, she is truly able to experience intimacy. As Lord Peter Wimsey says to his wife Harriet, "You have unmasked me, and loved me all the same."[2] Such intimacy is founded on grace and forgiveness.

Whole, sure, personal, and intimate relationships cannot be created in one's own strength. An absolutely sure promise can only come from an absolutely honest, absolutely powerful, and absolutely sacrificial person. A truly personal relationship can only be created between two perfect people. A perfect unity of body and soul can only come from someone who understands and controls both. And true intimacy can only occur between two people who are either perfect or perfectly able to forgive at all times.

Human Trust Needs a Cosmic Source: The Cosmic Covenant

Can two human beings expect honesty and trust from each other? Are we naive to think that we can depend on one another?

Yvette, a family friend of ours who died in 1992, was married to a man who shut her out of their bedroom, insisting that she sleep on the couch. He locked his dishes in a separate cupboard, ate on his own, and refused to give her any money, claiming that her dead mother had endowed her. He spent thousands on his own needs, purchasing a powerful motorcycle and a camping van in which he would travel for six months out of the year. He took the lightbulbs out of the chandelier, which hung from a high, vaulted ceiling, then locked the ladder in the garage so Yvette couldn't put in new bulbs.

On Christmas morning, Yvette went into her kitchen to find a skull and crossbones spray-painted on her wall. The skull sported a full head of curly blond hair, while a huge set of painted blue eyes peered down from above. (Yvette had curly blond hair and her husband's eyes were blue.) This man was not worthy of the trust Yvette had given him and was in breach of contract with a faithful wife.

Women are not the only ones to suffer from breach of contract. Men cannot trust women who manipulate them or take advantage of their willingness to be vulnerable. Women can be sneaky, controlling, and destructive. One woman I met told me that she deliberately stayed overweight as a way of avoiding sex with her husband. She knew she was unattractive, but she did it on purpose.

If men can't trust women, and women can't trust men, what hope is there for lasting relationships? As the Bible puts it: "They utter mere words; with empty oaths they make covenants; so judgment springs up like poisonous weeds in the furrows of the field" (Hos. 10:4 ESV). Such words fit our litigious society. Divorce lawyers thrive on the disputes and breaches of faith between husbands and wives. Many argue that there is no hope. A resigned bitterness reigns about male-female relationships.

But it is possible for a man and a woman to establish trust. The key is to bring to the relationship a solidity drawn not from each other but from an outside source. There is only one completely trustworthy source of wholeness, personal commitment, and intimacy. That source is the creative One who formed the world to reflect such qualities, found before human existence only in the Creator. We are all capable of covenant because we are made in the image of a Person who keeps covenant with us. The One who made us knows us. It is from that Creator that we can learn commitment, fidelity, honesty, and sacrificial love.

Of course, whether we admit it or not, we all rely on this source for any hope of human relationship. However, those who consciously rely on the Creator for the strength, humility, and love to live out their own marriage covenants (or other human covenantal relationships) will construct stronger bonds than those who are borrowing from the reserve of qualities they do not respect or claim as their own.

The Christian understands the basic order that God has worked into this world and receives the power to overcome evil, which has twisted that order, making a parody of it. For us to understand the limited covenant a woman makes with a man in marriage, we must understand that such a covenant is only a shadow of the Great Covenant.

Family Covenant Based on God the Creator's Nature

Unbreakable—"I Am Who I Am"

God made a covenant with His creatures. There is a great cosmological arrangement, a contract with the universe that carries promises and consequences. When two human beings enter into an arrangement, they seal it before some court or authority that will administer justice should something go wrong. However, God can submit Himself to no higher authority or judge. He can swear by nothing greater than Himself. As one Bible writer argues, men have to swear by something greater than themselves. Such an oath (in a court of law, for example) is binding and ends disputes. But God can only guarantee His promise by His own oath, which is our hope—a sure and firm anchor of the soul (Heb. 6:16–19).

God wrote a contract with His world and His people and put His signature on it. He makes promises and accepts the consequences of any breach of contract. Since God cannot appeal to some higher authority to adjudicate His promise, it must be His own nature and His own word promise that provide the unshakable foundation for the cosmic covenant. God is the only Father who can say, "Just because I say so." The uniquely true and perfect nature of God and His oath, sworn on His own being and name, serves as the court of justice for all human relationships. That justice is made clear to us in a written contract that God signed first with His "finger" on Mt. Sinai, when Moses went up the mountain to receive God's law.[3] Later, He signs the contract with His blood, when Jesus lays His life down in payment for our breach of contract with God.

When we understand and commit to the terms of the *cosmic* contract, we begin to understand the implications of the *lesser* contracts, since they are all intimately related in purpose and function to the universal covenant. God proves His trustworthiness and His personal commitment to His people first by His contract to uphold creation, secondly by His written promises, and finally by His willingness to pay the consequences when we broke the contract.

The stunning truth is that God takes the consequences of the broken contract, even though it was His people who were unfaithful. God signed off on promises to bless and protect His people, and they signed off on His law, repeatedly promising fidelity to their Creator and God. However, they failed abysmally and were subject to the penalties lined out in the fine print. But God extends mercy anyway. He submits to the ruinous penalties of His own covenant. He enters creation and submits Himself not only to the limitations of the flesh, but to moral horror in which humanity lives. While fulfilling for us the cosmic contract, Christ paid the penalty we deserved for breaching it and then conquered death, proving His power to affect real change in the world. He paved the way for His people to relate in true fidelity and honesty. It is only on the basis of His work that we can hope for good marriages.

Separate—Face-to-Face

In the person and nature of God exists not only the closeness, but also the separateness of persons that exists in a marriage. Marriage is only a created hint of the Trinity and is not a direct parallel, but it shows us something of the nature of God Himself. In God the Father is authority, initiating love, creative power, and inherent compassion. In God the Son we see the expression of the Father, equal in being, yet in submission to the Father's will (Heb. 1:2–3). The Son expresses the Father's glory, gives the Father glory, and receives the Father's glory. The Spirit is the great communicator, the heart-changer, who reveals the nature of God, convinces of sin, shows the beauty of God's righteousness, reveals the truth of God's Word, guides, urges, counsels, conquers, and woos on behalf of the Father and the Son.

The equality of person-ness and the separateness of functions is one of the great beauties and mysteries of the Trinity. I do not pretend to wrap my small mind around this infinite treasure, but one thing I know: God created structures in this universe to help us understand who He is. The separateness and equality of people in a family—the male as husband and father, the female as wife and mother, and children of both sexes as equal reflections of both the mother and the father, yet separate individuals in subjection to their parents—these human relationships, as mysterious as they are on a human level, also reflect the greater depth and breadth of love expressed in the fathomless Trinity.

United

In that "God-family" relationship of triune perfection we have the source of infinite love, of absolute communion, of indivisible fidelity, of burning honesty, of intense joy and boundless peace. The peoples of the twenty-first century have a huge longing for global unity. We all sense that oneness is necessary if our world is to make sense. In the Trinity we find ultimate unity, the basis for human unity. Jesus prays to the Father for His disciples, "Holy Father, protect them by Your name that You have given Me, so that they may be one as We are one" (John 17:11). Christians have a basis for maintaining their identity, yet finding true unity with one another. And a Christian man and his wife have this same unity/identity foundation laid for them in their marriage.

We are created for relationship with our Creator first of all, and then also for relationship with other human beings. God is a relational being. Within His nature He was already communicating, loving, initiating, responding, rejoicing, and experiencing community before human beings ever existed. He did not create man because He was lonely.

The first human relationship God created was that of husband and wife. God did not need the vows of the man to the woman or the woman to the man, promising fidelity to each other. He created that first male-female relationship as a *de facto* marriage. Adam's faithfulness to God implied a faithfulness not only to his role as caretaker of creation but also to the woman whom God created and gave to him. And Eve's faithfulness to God implies a faithfulness to the man already created. We were created already in relationship to God, already in relationship to one another, male and female.

From the context of marriage, all other human relationships emerged. No sooner were there two humans than there was a relationship between them. Here we find no independent careers traced by Adam and Eve's creativity and ambition. They do not choose each other out of their own wisdom and initiative. Marriage was the air they breathed from the moment Eve existed.

Godlike

God has set us in families. Says the poet King David, "Sing to God . . . a father to the fatherless, a defender of widows. . . . God sets the lonely in families" (Ps. 68:4–6 NIV). In the New Testament, the apostle Paul says, "I bow my knees before the Father, from whom every family [all fatherhood] in heaven and on earth is named" (Eph. 3:14). (Notice the heavenly model for fatherhood in this verse.) God has placed family structures in the world for our human benefit but also to show us a hint of the beauty of the Trinity, because in God's person are caught up all the glories of personal relationship, communion, communication, fellowship, love, and face-to-faceness.

Male and Female Based on God the Creator's Nature

Separate

God the Creator takes great joy in separating things. We all love to think of God as the God of unity. But the unity that God creates depends on His first having made distinctions. I cannot be united with my husband if my husband is not a separate person. I have to look him in the eye to know him and to be known by him. The Bible's account of creation repeats over and over the separating work of God. God distinguishes the night from the day, the sea from the dry land, the heavens from the earth. The very first separation is that between the Creator and the creature. He does not locate Himself in the creation, making it a spatially identifiable part of Himself. The creation is not God. It is other than God. God relates to us in our separateness from Him. God also creates relationships between mankind and animals, between mankind and the plants, and between males and females. Those relationships are also distinct from one another. We relate differently to a tulip than to a friend.

God sets each species apart to produce after its own kind. This notion of separateness distinguishes the Christian faith from many expressions of spirituality that find their culmination in an ultimate experience of oneness with the creation itself. Such spiritual experiences glory in erasing a sense of personal distinction.

In *The Color Purple*, for example, Alice Walker's character, the bi-sexual Shug, describes the experience of moving away from this God who is separate to a new god: "My first step from the old white man was trees. Then air. Then birds. Then other people. But one day when I was sitting quiet and feeling like a motherless child, which I was, it come to me: that feeling of being part of everything, not separate at all. I knew that if I cut a tree, my arm would bleed. And I laughed and I cried and I run all around the house. I knew just what it was. In fact, when it happens, you can't miss it."[4]

Shug has a powerful, mystical conversion experience. She is turning away from the separate God, who is outside the universe, to a new understanding. She and the tree and God are all one and the same. Her experience of unity with the tree she compares to a mystical/sexual union—an absolute orgasm with the universe. The loneliness and longing and separateness that all of us feel have been answered for Shug by a spiritual satisfaction, that she is one with the tree. Such mystical spiritual experiences of oneness are highly revered in the "new spirituality" of the twenty-first century.

However, people seek unity with the wrong things. What they *think* they are separated from is not what they are *really* separated from. Shug's desperate loneliness and her desire to be "connected" is right. However, she defines God's demands on her life as the force that separates her from unity with the soul of life. Her real separation is not from creation, but from the Creator. She eliminates the tension of His holy demands by wiping Him out of her universe. However, only by approaching and dealing with His judgment could she get past the separation barrier.

True unity *requires* separateness. Just as a couple who marries finds union without the destruction of their individuality, so unity with the Creator brings our nature into clearer focus. There are absolutes in God's creation which must not be changed if we are to know ourselves, know our Creator, and find our place in His universe. Shug, the animals, and the trees are *not* God. God has authority over us and dictates the limits of our being.

Separate and Subject

The Christian starts at another point entirely. We are God's creatures, functioning within the cosmic contract. We are created not only *separate* but *subject*. The definition of our life's goal is given to us by God Himself: "to bring all things in heaven and on earth together under one head, even Christ" (Eph. 1:10 NIV). You can see how antithetical are the goals of the Christian and those of Alice Walker's character. The Christian woman finds her identity and fulfillment in recognizing and accepting the separateness of her created state. She rejoices in it and finds union with God by subjecting herself to Him as Creator and Father, and by receiving His loving care and protection. Shug finds identity and fulfillment in refusing that separateness and rejecting her created state. She rejoices in her imagined union with God and elevates herself to an uncreated state, but she will ultimately know only darkness, futility, and disillusionment.

Like many of us, Shug tries to redefine God according to her own desires and whims. If there really is a Creator, then it is He who defines us, not *vice versa*. Part of our difficulty in determining the way we think about men and women and about their relationship with God is that we begin with our own definitions of what we expect. We end up creating God in our own image rather than accepting the fact that we are made in His.

The Christian faith offers definitions from the outside, so to speak. We live our lives according to rules written by the Creator, not according to our own house rules. These rules and definitions are not beyond our understanding, but they are not of our making. The Great Maker, the author of the cosmic contract, communicates with us and tells us who we are. Moses bragged about Him in these words: "What other nation is so great as to have their gods near them the way the LORD our God is near us whenever we pray to him?" (Deut. 4:7 NIV) And the apostle Paul said something similar when he addressed a forum of Greek philosophers in Athens: "The God who made the world and everything in it—He is Lord of heaven and earth. . . . From one man He has made every nation of men . . . and has determined . . . the boundaries of where they live, so that they might seek God, and perhaps . . . reach out and find Him, though He is not far from each one of us" (Acts 17:24–27).

Christians live in a connected universe. The created structures are God-given and show us the God who defines the world and our place in it. We can understand the differences between men and women as well as their relationships with each other only by conforming ourselves to the master plan. Fortunately, we are not left in the dark about the plan. When we reach out to God, we find Him, as He promised. God doesn't hide, but He tells us in His world and in His Word who He is. If you don't know what you think about God, let me ask you to enter a state of "suspension" as you read on. You may have suffered because of cruel or selfish men. Your father may have let you down. I'm asking you to begin thinking that there might exist, just maybe, a true Father for you—someone who not only cares about you, but who has the power to protect you and a bottomless reserve of love to give you all you need and desire as a woman.

In a society soaked in feminism, what God tells us about a woman's identity may at first seem obnoxious, old-fashioned, and perhaps even repressive. But this wise Father only wants our joy and fulfillment. Let's see how He answers Jakki's question: "What's a woman?"

■ ■ ■

Discussion Questions

1. Have you ever felt betrayed or let down by a man?

2. Can you trust the people with whom you have the most intimate relationships? Why? Why not?

3. In what ways do you feel "separate" from other people or from God? Is it a fearful sense of loneliness or a confident sense of identity?

4. Are you dependent on other people? Is this good or bad?

5. How do you define "trust"?

6. Do you trust other women? Why or why not?

7. Do you trust yourself?

8. Do you know someone utterly trustworthy?

9. How do you define God? Can you trust your God?

10. What are some reasons why we find it hard to trust God, even if we believe Him to be completely trustworthy?

■ ■ ■

Resources

Arthur, Kay. *Our Covenant God: Learning to Trust Him.* New York: WaterBrook Press, 1999.

Frame, John. *The Doctrine of God.* Phillipsburg, N.J.: P&R, 2002.

Horton, Michael S. *Putting Amazing Back into Grace.* Ann Arbor, Mich.: Baker, 1994.

Kassian, Mary. *In My Father's House: Women Relating to God as Father.* Nashville: LifeWay, 1999.

Lewis, Nathan. *In Search of Satisfaction.* Evergreen Church, 2002.

Olyott, Stuart. *What the Bible Teaches about the Trinity.* Darlington, England: Evangelical Press, n.d.

Packer, J. I. *Knowing God.* Leicester, England: InterVarsity, 1993.

Piper, John. *Desiring God.* Sisters, Ore.: Multnomah, 2003.

Short, John-Rendle. *Man in the Image of God.* www.answersingenesis .org/ Docs/3761.asp.

*[W]here His living image, like Him within and without, made by
His own bare hands out of the depth of divine artistry, His masterpiece
of self portraiture coming forth from His workshop to delight all worlds,
walked and spoke, it could never be taken for more than an image.
Nay, the very beauty of it lay in the certainty that it was a copy, like and
not the same, a rhyme, an exquisite reverberation of untreated music
prolonged in a created medium.*

—C. S. LEWIS, ON ADAM'S
CREATION

3

■ ■ ■ ■ ■

Jakki's Question

THE QUEEN OF UNDERLAND in C. S. Lewis's book, *The Silver Chair,*
tries to persuade Puddleglum, Prince Rilian, Jill Pole, and Eustace
Scrubb that her dark, underground world, where she holds them captive, is the only world that exists. The three friends, under the spell of
the queen's music and the magic of a powder she has thrown on the fire,
struggle to clear their heads and to affirm the reality of the world they
know by seizing on their memory of the sun. "Then came the Witch's
voice, cooing softly, 'What is this sun that you speak of? . . . What is it
like?' . . . 'You see that lamp,' replies the Prince. 'Now that thing which
we call the sun is like the lamp, only far greater and brighter.' The queen
laughs. 'When you try to think out clearly what this sun must be, you
can only tell me it is like the lamp. Your sun is a dream.'"[1]

Fortunately, Puddleglum, the children's pessimistic but faithful guide, has the good sense to resist the queen's sly logic. By stamping out her fire with his foot, he brings Jill and Eustace back to their senses.

The Image of God in Man

God is not just a huge lamp. The lamp is only *like* the sun. When we try to imagine what God is like, we sometimes fall into the trap the witch was proposing to the enchanted travelers. We take what we as human beings know and see and project our knowledge of them on to God. We reason that if both men and women are in God's image, then God's image must be an amalgam of maleness and femaleness. But God's person is infinitely broader, deeper, greater, and more mysterious than the "person-ness" of human beings.

Both men and women reflect God's nature, and God makes a special love contract with them, because, unlike anything else in His creation, they are "in His image." That human reflection of God is valid and good, but it is only the lamp, not the sun. To say that humankind is created in the image of God, male and female, is not to say that God is both "male and female," some kind of magnified, bodiless androgyne.[2] Our "male and female" qualities reflect something of who God is. God is the sun in the sky, and humans are the lamp in the underworld.

We have friends who visited the Grand Canyon with us. As we stood, overwhelmed by the exquisite, breathtaking immensity of the shadows, the delicate and dramatic colors of the huge cliffs, the broad and soaring sky, we began to talk about God. How could we help it? In our discussion our friends realized that we Christians had the sense of belonging personally to the God who made such splendor. However, when we spoke of God as a Person, one of them protested: "That would make God too small!"

Our friend was recreating God in the image of the only "persons" we know—humans. When we say God is personal, we do not mean He has the limitations of a human person. God has qualities that will never be true of us. He is eternal, uncreated, infinitely powerful, and wise. He made everything that exists and knows everything about us. But in other ways, we *are* like God. We are creative, morally sensitive, and able to enjoy beauty. We can communicate verbally, sing, laugh, and love others. We can truly know God, though not exhaustively.

God defines the rules of the game of life. He sets the boundaries of our lives and determines what it takes to succeed. He is the reference point for all our questions and the arbiter of all disputes. We don't get to pick what color piece we want on the board. God placed His image in us when He created us, and He is the only one who can restore the picture that was spoiled by the very first people to live on earth. If it is true that God made us and defines who we are, then Jakki's question, "What's a woman?" can only be answered by God. Woman was His idea. To find out how we as women can be true to our feminine nature, we have to understand why God made us to start with. What's the point of men and women? How are they different, and how can we be true to ourselves as males or females?

The Image, Male and Female

As I mentioned briefly in chapter 2, when God made the universe, He separated the heavens from the earth, night from day, land from water. He separated one kind of animal from another, so that elephants bear elephants, while weasels bear weasels. He separated male from female. God did not create one uniform, sexless human being, then clone it to create the human race. He made a binary (male/female) version of His image that would come together to produce after their own kind. Adam and Eve are of the same kind but distinct, as male and female.[3]

The Bible clearly explains that both men and women are in God's image: "On the day that God created man, He made him in the likeness of God; He created them male and female. When they were created, He blessed them and called them man" (Gen. 5:2).

The Image in Adam

God created men and women equal, yet different. The Bible is full of evidence that God values women as much as He values men. They are of the same substance. Both are in God's image (Gen. 1:27). Both are commissioned to rule the earth and to fill it (Gen. 1:28). Both answer to God for sin. Both exercise faith in looking to the future promise of salvation. Both, by faithfully fulfilling their separate roles, participate in the fulfillment of the promise that God makes to provide a Savior (the promised progeny, the Messiah). Both participate in the grand love contract (sometimes called the "covenant of grace") signed into effect by Jesus' death and resurrection (Gal. 3:28; 1 Pet. 3:7). Both receive the gift of God's Spirit and are born into God's family by faith. Both receive spiritual gifts with which they serve Christ, His church, and the world.

Nonetheless, Adam is given a representative place as head of his home and head of the human race. On Adam's shoulders falls the ultimate responsibility for the rebellion in the garden,[4] even though it was Eve's initiative that began the process. The leadership and authority exercised by a man over his wife and children is evident in that he was created first and was given primary responsibility for the human race.[5] It was to Adam that God first gave the job of tending and keeping the garden. It was to Adam that God entrusted the all-important command not to eat of the tree of the knowledge of good and evil. It was to Adam that God gave the responsibility of naming the animals, and even of naming his wife. It was from Adam's rib that the woman was created.

This "firstness" of Adam is not just the fact that he was made before Eve. It represents a primacy of function. Adam's representation prepares us for another Adam whose representative role will also be crucial for humanity. Later in history will come a new man, who will serve as our representative and will be the first of "many brothers,"[6] the head of a new human family.

The Image in Eve

The drama with which God introduces Adam to his new wife is replayed in every marriage ceremony. A man doesn't want to see his wife in her wedding dress until the moment she walks down the aisle. The stunning surprise of her beauty is a part of the drama of a wedding. But Adam had never been to a wedding. In fact, he had never seen a woman before. Adam had yet to see any creature truly like him.

In his God-given task of naming the animals, Adam had gone through the entire acreage of the Eden Zoological and Botanical Gardens; he had to be well aware of the male-female nature of things. Perhaps he had witnessed a glorious all-species mating display, in which the male and female of each animal triumphantly discovered each other. Who can say? But when Adam had named all the animals, he still had found no suitable partner. Not one of these creatures was worth a second look. They were obviously not his type, not his "kind"! (This is a reminder to us that bestiality was never God's idea.)

Having established this truth firmly in Adam's mind and spirit, God puts him into a deep sleep. God sometimes takes a man out of action in this way in the Bible. The creature worthy to be Adam's precious and beautiful helper is all of God's doing, not of Adam's. Adam doesn't enter desirable statistics in a dating profile. He doesn't know what he needs or wants, since he could not have thought up a woman. God doesn't even allow Adam to watch the operation under local anesthetic. His wife is a miracle, an undeserved gift from God, designed perfectly for his needs, and he for hers; a glorious alternative human being, so like, yet so unlike, him. He does not look at her in the same way he looked at the animals. He doesn't need to reflect before bursting out with an exclamation of enthusiasm. Her beauty and perfection evoke in him the Hebrew equivalent of "Whoa!" He is stunned. Blown away.

The account of the creation of the woman leaves before us a straightforward fact: the woman was created to bring God glory by helping and assisting the man. This is the reason she was made, the earthly definition of her existence. You can accept it or reject it, but the text is clear. The male-female combination, this powerful and perfect, united couple, has a job to do. The job description is now handed to the couple, who are the only candidates. They are perfectly suited to it because together they are to subdue and fill the earth—a job neither could do alone.

Adam and Eve are physically, emotionally, and spiritually different in their reactions, instincts, thought patterns, and ways of approaching life, yet they are also the same. They are both of equal value to God and both fully in His image. When their first child arrives, they will understand that this tiny creature, who in so many ways looks neither like Adam nor Eve, is also in God's image, even though he was not created full-grown, as were his parents. Unfortunately, this first "birthed" human will not share something Adam and Eve both had at the beginning—perfection.

The Image and the Curse

Adam and Eve start out in relationships of absolute comfort, trust, and satisfaction. Eve has everything a woman could want. Good relationships with men—she had a perfect husband, a Father like no other (heavenly!), and sons not only promised but commanded. Good relationships with women—not yet, but coming. A place to call home—she is mistress of the Garden of Eden with the fellowship of animals, Adam, and God Himself to make it truly cozy. Children—coming soon. Promised. Value in the world—Eve is the *only* woman in the world! She couldn't have been anymore valuable. The future of the entire universe hangs on her help to Adam in subduing the world and filling it with children. She might be defined as the queen of utopia.

So what happens? I'm afraid Eve does what we will see many women doing as we look at their stories in this book. She tries to improve on God's plan by using her own clever strategies. Eve's attempt to become *more* like God (a laudable goal and one that God Himself would have accomplished for her) backfires, and she becomes very *unlike* God. The power and beauty of her Godlikeness is put to the service of defaming God, stealing His honor for another, and drawing her husband away from his fidelity to God's clear, spoken commands.

After the Fall, man begins using all his glory and gifts to create a name for himself rather than honoring God's name: "Let us build ourselves a city, with a tower that reaches to the heavens, so that we may make a name for ourselves" (Gen. 11:4 NIV). God takes the project seriously, since fallen humans still possess power and ability: "If as one people speaking the same language they have begun to do this, then nothing they plan to do will be impossible for them" (Gen. 11:6 NIV) Without the constraining mercies of God that often frustrate wicked plans, men in God's image create a fearful and powerful unity for evil, the effects of which we have seen over and over in our cruel and war-torn world.[7]

In their eager desire to create a better world, Adam and Eve create the terrain for pollution, jealousy, anarchy, despotism, futility, sickness, and, above all, death. They break the unity of the God-man relationship, betraying the trust that God has given them. They break the contract. The stench of their moral and physical decay makes it impossible for them to come before their Creator naked and without shame. The delighted "Whoa!" that Adam spontaneously shouted at his first sight of the stunning, naked Eve now becomes a groan of despair. The first humans begin a frantic search for something behind which they can hide—from each other but also from God. Their own attempts to cover themselves with leaves are laughable. God now clothes the guilty pair in animal skins. We see in this first sacrifice, performed by God Himself on behalf of His human images, the first glimpses of what it will cost to draw men back into communion with each other and with their Creator.[8]

Their eviction from the garden, though a punishment, is also an act of mercy on God's part. He evicts them so they cannot make permanent their state of sin and decay by eating the fruit of the tree of life. God Himself will provide that fruit later, in His own way, in His own plan. They will only be allowed to eat of it once He has dealt with their rebellion. Into God's world has come strife and hatred. A cosmic war has begun between the offspring of the woman and the power of the evil one, the tempter.

The desperate struggle will affect both male and female. Before the first woman has even had a child, childbirth is placed under heavy constraints of suffering, and the relationship between the male and female image is also broken. The woman will now desire to "have" her husband, just as sin crouched at the door, desiring to pounce on Cain.[9] The male will try, in revenge, to dominate, thus twisting his God-given job of care into a prideful, selfish tyranny.

When Adam and Eve sin, they bring a direct curse on the devil and on the earth. The ground will still produce its fruit for the benefit of man's body, but he will have to work hard to sow seed and harvest its fruits. The fertile body of the woman will still produce fruit for the salvation of man's soul, though such fruit will come with great pain to body and soul, and with hard work. In the catastrophe of the Fall, we feel the empty meaninglessness of the world as we know it: "Everything is meaningless. What does man gain from all his labor at which he toils under the sun?" (Eccles. 1:2–3 NIV).

But there is hope. God shows incredible mercy to His beloved offspring.[10] The curse on the serpent holds blessing for the human race, because the serpent has not won the final victory. God's mercy extends the conflict, holding back the sun, so to speak, so night will not fall until the final Joshua has victory over all of God's enemies (see Josh. 10:12–13).

Who is the unlikely hero of the battle? None other than the seed of the woman! How comforting for Eve, who doubtless realized with a black hollow in the pit of her stomach that her arrogance and pride was the source of all the misery that had befallen the brand-new race. God did not leave Adam and Eve to grovel in the cave of their fear and horror. He came searching, as He has done throughout history, seeking and saving us as we hide, hopeless and depressed, angry and defensive, in the shadows of our misery.

The image of God in man was not obliterated by Adam and Eve's sin, but it was transformed into a portrait of horror. One of my daughters is an excellent artist. In my living room are two portraits of her. One stands in full display, but the other is tucked behind a bookshelf.

The first was done for a school assignment. My theory on the missing mouth was that at the time she didn't yet know whose name she claimed and could not, therefore, confess "who" she was. Otherwise, it is a lovely likeness of her.

The one behind the bookshelf was done hastily, with angry, bold strokes, in a moment of defiance and despair. It was a good likeness of what she was for a time—an unhappy girl occasionally full of hatred and rebellion. We discovered that sketch one morning, propped up on our dining table, accompanied by a sheet on which were scrawled the words, "I hate you!" It is ugly, full of terror, repulsive, shocking. It still looks like her, but I don't display it in our living room. It carries with it the memory of trying days.

In our state of sin, we humans stare back at God, angry and sullen, stamping our feet, shouting "I hate you!" and causing our Father and Creator to recoil in horror and shock as He sees His reflection distorted, shattered, and leering. Eve herself experienced the same sense of horror as she watched her first son, Cain, murder Abel. The first child will not be the promised one, the Savior who restores life. He will be rather the first murderer, taking into his own angry hands the execution of the death sentence that had been passed on to the entire family of man.

Never has a son been more of a disappointment than Cain was to Adam and Eve. Never had any parents' hopes been higher or plunged lower. How desperately they must have wept in the despair of their black future. Some of you reading this book may be anguishing over the disappointment of a child who is not what you had hoped and expected. As one of my friends said, "Things were supposed to be sweet!" Eve would weep with you and put her arms around you. She understood the horror, the doubt, the grief.

The Sharper Image

How she and Adam must have puzzled over the promise, and over God's actions after their sin. Adam knew that no animal was suited to be his mate or helper, yet God had sacrificed an animal to clothe them. How could this be? If an animal could not serve as a mate, how could it serve as a savior? The sacrifice, good as it was for physical clothing, was insufficient to clothe them spiritually. God had promised salvation through the seed of the woman, not through the seed and the blood of an animal. Would the blood of Abel be the blood that would cry from the ground and satisfy the justice of God? Yet Abel had not been chosen by God as a sacrifice. The blood of Abel did not cry out to God as atonement to cover the sin of the human race. It cried out, rather, for justice. That blood was not the blood that saved them, but the blood that sealed their guilt.

Eve must have wondered how her seed could ever save the human race. Perhaps she thought that a son of hers would have to be sacrificed as payment. She may have asked herself, "Should I give my firstborn for my transgression, the child of my body for my own sin?" (Mic. 6:7).[11]

How could any seed of Adam and Eve rescue the human race from death? That seed was doomed, because it was still in the body of Adam who was himself tainted by sin. All of Eve's children were automatically under the curse of sin and death, so how could one of her descendants ever serve as a perfect sacrifice and savior? No natural seed of Adam and Eve could fulfill God's promise, yet that promise one day became reality.

Just as we didn't stop loving our daughter when she was feeling so angry with us, so God didn't give up on the human race. God's promise of a Savior from Eve's womb was not fulfilled in Cain, or in Abel, but Eve would have a son through whose line a perfect man would one day be born. He could act as a sacrifice and bring hope of a renewed image of God. Eve, the woman, is crucial to God's plan. Without her, salvation would not have been possible.

In the arrangement God makes with His world, whether in the original creation structures or in the buy-back arrangement He concludes on our behalf, men and women each have important roles to play. God's binary version of human beings is not accidental. It is structurally crucial to the accomplishment of all His goals and plans, for when the Savior does arrive, He is a *man,* born of a *woman.*

To understand our place as women in God's world, we have to get the "big picture." We have to find out how the sun infuses the lamp with real light. God is the sun and men and women are the lamps that are the image of the sun. It is the Creator who made women who can tell us what we were meant to be and do. The wonderful thing is that God has told us these things. He doesn't hide the truth from us, but tells us clearly in His Word who He is and who we are. By examining the Bible, we can find God's glorious answer to the question: "What's a woman?"

■ ■ ■

Discussion Questions

1. How are humans like God, as He is described in the Bible? How are they unlike God?

2. How are men and women different? How are they alike?

3. How can we tell whether the differences we see between the sexes are only cultural and not created by God?

4. How is the image of God "sharpened" or improved for Christians, as over against Adam and Eve's understanding of image?

5. Does the Bible define what a woman is? If so, where?

6. How was Eve to help Adam? What is she to help him do?

7. Are all women supposed to help all men?

8. The Bible makes it obvious that men are supposed to help women as well as women helping men. In what ways does a man's help for his wife differ from a wife's help for her husband?

9. Do you resent being a woman? If so, in what areas?

10. Practically speaking, as a Christian, how could you be more womanly? Be sure to think about the Bible's standards, not necessarily your cultural standards.

■ ■ ■

Resources

Crabb, Larry. *Men and Women: Enjoying the Difference.* Grand Rapids: Zondervan, 1991.

———. *The Silence of Adam: Becoming Men of Courage in a World of Chaos.* Grand Rapids: Zondervan, 1998.

Doriani, Dan. *The Life of a God-Made Man: Becoming a Man After God's Heart.* Wheaton, Ill.: Crossway, 2001.

Fitzpatrick, Elyse. *Helper by Design.* Chicago: Moody Publishers, 2003.

Hoekema, Anthony. *Created in God's Image.* Chicago: Eerdmans, 1994.

Hunt, Susan. *By Design: God's Distinctive Calling for Women.* Wheaton, Ill.: Crossway, 1994.

Hurley, James B. *Man and Woman in Biblical Perspective.* Leicester, England: InterVarsity, 1981.

Kassian, Mary. *Women, Creation and the Fall.* Wheaton, Ill.: Crossway, 1990.

MacArthur, John, Jr. *Different By Design: Discovering God's Will for Today's Man and Woman.* Colorado Springs, Colo.: Chariot, Victor Books, 1994.

Neuer, Werner. *Man and Woman in Christian Perspective.* Trans. Gordon Wenham. Wheaton, Ill.: Crossway, 1991.

Packer, J. I. "Reflected Glory: What does Genesis mean by man being made in the image of God?" *Christianity Today.* December 2003. Can be read online at www.christianitytoday.com/ct/2003/012/20.56.html.

Piper, John and Wayne Grudem, eds. *Recovering Biblical Manhood and Womanhood: A Response to Evangelical Feminism.* Wheaton, Ill.: Crossway, 1991. See especially John Frame's chapter, "The Image of God in Man," available also online at www. leaderu.com/orgs/cbmw/rbmw/chapter12.html.

Rainbow, Paul. *Orthodox Trinitarianism and Evangelical Feminism.* Booklet, available at www.cbmw.org.

Strauch, Alexander. *Men and Women: Equal Yet Different: A Brief Study of the Biblical Passages on Gender.* Littleton, Colo.: Lewis and Roth, 1999.

Ware, Bruce. *Tampering with the Trinity: Does the Son Submit to His Father?* Booklet, available at www.cbmw.org.

Beginning with Moses and all the Prophets, [Jesus] interpreted to them in all the Scriptures the things concerning himself.

—LUKE 24:27 ESV

4

The Bible

OLD TESTAMENT WOMEN ARE plentiful and varied. Abraham's wife Sarah has her first baby at the age of ninety. Jael drives a tent peg into the temple of an enemy general. The young girl Miriam negotiates a deal with an Egyptian princess to keep her baby brother at home—and get paid for it! Rachel, Jacob's favorite wife, hides idols under a saddle and refuses to rise, under pretext that she is having her period. What do we make of such obscure stories, which often seem irrelevant to life in the twenty-first century?

In the last chapter, we saw that the God who created woman is the only One who has the right to define her. God alone truly understands how we are to function in our sexual identities. But God doesn't tease us by keeping such knowledge to Himself. He communicates it to us in the Bible, though we often misread His message. I heard a discussion of the book of Esther, for example, on National Public Radio, that came to a grand, moralistic conclusion: Women must combine in life the "no" of Vashti and the "yes" of Esther.[1] Such an approach is only one example of many poor suggestions for interpreting Old Testament stories.

How *are* we to interpret them? If we take all the Bible's characters as heroic examples, we would have to kill anyone who walks through our front door, as did the judge Jephthah in the book of Judges (Judg. 11:30–31) or cut up the corpse of a murder victim and ship the body parts by UPS all around the country, as did a Levite priest (Judg. 19:29). What principles help us understand what the Bible means for us today or how it relates to the issues of a woman's identity and role?

The Bible: Record of the Covenant

In preparing to write this book, I determined to listen through the entire Bible. As I pedaled at the fitness center, I rode through Eden and Egypt and wound my way along the paths of God's huge promises, Israel's stubborn infidelity, and the patient discipline that God exercised to lead them back to Him. I found myself scolding the people of Israel, "No! You're not going to do that again. Didn't you learn *anything* from what happened in the last chapter?" The stories are poignant. I cried along with David as he moaned, "Absalom, my son, my son! Would that I had died instead of you!" I was surprised to feel so moved by the gracious love of Boaz for Ruth, the gutsy wisdom of Abigail, and the humble vows of Job to receive both good and bad from the hand of God.

The powerful humility of Jesus intrigued me as I listened to the Gospels, trying to imagine the tension Jesus knew as He anticipated the cross. The disciples' transformation from confused, fearful bumblers to bold leaders is miraculous, and Paul's closely reasoned texts do not disguise his searing, passionate love for his Jewish brothers and his Gentile parishioners. God's grand story climaxes with a vision of the wedding reception to come, opening the window on a world so far beyond our comprehension that my breath was taken away and a wave of awe swept over me.

The Bible is an astounding library of books. Rich in variety, color, poetry, emotion, history, realistic situations, human drama, down-to-earth characters, and spiritual power, its writings span centuries and were written by scores of different authors. But the Bible is not only a fascinating anthology of literature. It has a central theme, which is a love story, the saga of God's courtship with His bride, leading to the final marriage between God and His people. How the bride fell into captivity, was rescued, and finally bought at the cost of the life of her suitor—this story has not yet concluded. The invitations to the wedding feast are still out. If you are reading this book today, you still have time to RSVP King Jesus' personalized invitation. This huge, cosmic romance concerns us all. Knowing the Bridegroom is our purpose in life. In one sense, we can accurately say that the whole Bible is a detailed marriage contract between God and His people.

For this reason, our understanding of both the Old and the New Testament is set into the context of marriage. Our place as women, our sexuality, and our family structures are all intimately linked with God's purposes in the world. The spiritual marriage between God and His bride cannot be extricated from our own personal marriages and relationships. God made marriage to show us what His love is like. God is pursuing a bride, seeking and saving us in order to make us His treasured wife. He has a home ready for us. The mortgage is paid for eternity. He will carry us over the threshold and delight in us forever. Understanding God's Word is the only way to find out how to get home.

The Bible: Torn Apart

We cannot understand the Old Testament without the New Testament or the New Testament without the Old Testament. Unfortunately, Christians have abandoned the study of the Old Testament. Preachers use sagas from it for moral purposes or a psalm to echo our feelings, but they rarely preach through an Old Testament book.[2]

Why have Christians abandoned the first half of their Bible? Perhaps we are so hooked on grace that Old Testament law disturbs us. Perhaps a world trying to achieve global peace cannot accept accounts of ancient wars. Perhaps our weakened educational standards have not equipped us to study more complex books. One major reason for avoiding the Old Testament is its perceived denigration of women. To solve their discomfort in this area, some Bible scholars simply decide to read the Old Testament texts "against the grain,"[3] or to invent imaginary texts about Bible events, this time written from the female perspective. We have such works as the *Chronicles of Noah and Her Sisters: Genesis and Exodus According to Women.*[4]

Feminism fights Paul's letters even harder than it does the Old Testament. Liberals in general don't much like Paul; or if they like him, it is out of curiosity for such a fascinating, pathetic, and arrogant woman-hater. They willingly cite the passage on love, while studiously avoiding other texts. The average Christian has abandoned the Old Testament, hesitates to defend the politically incorrect sections of Paul's letters, and doesn't dare tackle Revelation, which is difficult and controversial.

This leaves us with the four Gospels, and a few other New Testament books. Theologians like those of the Jesus Seminar argue, with the full power of media support, that the Jesus painted in the Synoptic Gospels is only one version of Jesus and a slanted one at that. They have put out a volume called *The Five Gospels,*[5] which includes the gnostic Gospel of Thomas. Using the red-letter principle, they categorize the texts of all five Gospels by color: black for what Jesus surely never said; gray for what He probably didn't say; pink for what He probably *did* say, and red for what He *definitely* said. Would it be a surprise to discover that the pinks and reds are in the gnostic Gospel of Thomas, while the blacks and grays are mostly in the Gospel of John?

The Jesus Seminar's attack on the unity and veracity of the Scriptures has recently hit the mass markets in the form of a best-selling novel, the *Da Vinci Code,* which casts doubt on the formation of the canon and elevates gnostic spirituality as an ideal. This book and similar subtle but fierce attacks have caught Christians off guard. Not many know how to defend their Bible.[6]

The Bible: Ignored

Christians can't defend the Bible because we no longer know it well. During the persecution of the Huguenots, two little girls defeated an archbishop in arguing from the Scriptures about whether there were two or seven sacraments. One theologian, setting out a regimen for the education of a seven-year-old girl, insisted that she memorize the entire Psalter. Long ago, in American schools, Bible verses were used for reading practice, and biblical imagery was a regular part of our literature and media citations. Now, our culture will not allow the Ten Commandments to hang on the walls of our public buildings.

If you ask a child today which story tells of a hero swallowed by a great fish, he will reply *Pinocchio* or *Finding Nemo.* Children no longer know of Jonah, Noah, Abraham, or Paul. Adults fare no better. An American presidential candidate says his favorite New Testament book is the book of Job! Christian parents get no natural help in teaching biblical values to their children. In fact, two Protestant Bible teachers are quoted as finding the Bible too reactionary for their children to read.[7]

Church Bible study groups use books about the Bible rather than the Bible itself, though some movements have made headway in getting Christians back into their Bibles. Certain churches and Christian schools still insist on memory work and real Bible instruction. But let's assume that you *want* to study the Bible. How do you know what lessons to draw from it? What do we make of talking donkeys and chopped-up concubines?

The Bible: Misinterpreted

Christians have used some odd methods to understand and apply Bible truths. Some continue in the "close your eyes, open your Bible, and point at a verse" approach. The classic joke about this method tells of a man who stabbed at the verse, "Judas went and hanged himself." Not seeing how this was applicable to his life, he tried again and fell on the verse, "Go thou, and do likewise." We would never use another book this way. Christians are tempted by such a method because they know that the Word of God has life-directing power. In a misguided attempt to understand and benefit from that power, they use their Bibles as a kind of mystical horoscope. God "tells" them all kinds of things when they consult the Bible each morning.

Another mistake is to make careless, specific applications of scriptural promises to a subset of God's people. Americans are prone to assuming that the promises given to God's people in the Bible apply to their own "chosen" country. For any political or ethnic entity to appropriate for its own national group the promises God made to His global people is to misunderstand Jesus' teachings about the nature of the church.

In addition to the personal-mystical mistake and the political equivalent mistake, we often see the moralistic mistake. Understanding the Bible becomes a task of forcing certain behaviors on people. Such moralism is not modern. The Pharisees in Jesus' time used God's commands to make themselves look good while breaking the true intention of the law. For example, they had worked out a clever system to avoid supporting their elderly parents. Using Old Testament law, they claimed to dedicate all their belongings to the Lord, so they wouldn't have to pay for the upkeep of a parent. Jesus sees through their misuse of the law: "Hypocrites! Isaiah prophesied correctly about you when he said: These people honor Me with their lips, but their heart is far from Me" (Matt. 15:7–8).

We have all met such Pharisees in our lives. We see the Pharisee in a man who uses his God-given authority in the home to make his children into personal slaves. We see the Pharisee in a woman who uses the Bible's insistence on modesty as an excuse to neglect her husband's sexual needs. We see the Pharisee in a hard-hearted Christian who refuses to forgive a Christian brother because he has not sufficiently repented.

Some moralism comes from ignorance of good study methods. The Sunday school teacher tells the story of David's bravery in fighting a bear and a lion, and then instructs the children to be brave when the scary dog next door frightens their baby sister. Such a direct moral application of the story, though well-intentioned, misses the point entirely.

The story of David's unlikely victory underlines his weakness and the fact that it is only by faith in the power of God that David is able to wrestle with carnivores or bring down Goliath. Without God's power and without His champion, we are helpless to defeat our enemies. That David approached Goliath in faith alone is proof that the savior of the nation is not a savior because of his courage or strength, but because God steps in and accomplishes salvation. From God alone comes salvation.

So what principles *should* guide our biblical interpretation and application as we examine the specifics of the Bible's teaching on the role and identity of women?

Looking at Genre

Highly qualified theologians have discussed how to study the Bible. I hesitate to deal with the subject in one chapter, but we do have to think about it briefly, because so many people are dealing with the women's issue using questionable approaches to Bible interpretation. In my local Christian newspaper I saw an ad inviting "women of divine purpose" to a conference taught by three women pastors. The advertisement took a piece of a verse from Judges and quoted it this way: "There were no warriors in Israel until I, Deborah, arose."

I was a little puzzled as I read that verse, since I had never remembered Deborah being compared to a warrior. Sure enough, when I checked the text (with the help of my wonderful computer program), I found that none of the normal Bible translations use the word *warrior*. In fact, that word is used in the Bible only in this verse. Most translations use something like "villagers" ("The *villagers* ceased in Israel; they ceased to be until I arose; I, Deborah, arose as a mother in Israel" [Judg. 5:7 ESV], author's italics).

On the basis of one obscure word, probably poorly translated, an entire attitude is being set about a woman's role in God's kingdom. We will discuss Deborah's place, so don't become impatient now. But let us realize how important it is to understand and apply valid study methods, or we will come out with faulty results. Here are a few simple rules for good interpretation.

One basic rule in Bible interpretation is to take the genre of the piece into account. Genre means the category of literature of a work. Poetry, for example, was not intended to teach us scientific analysis. For example, Psalm 78:65 says, "Then the Lord awoke as if from sleep, like a warrior from the effects of wine." This does not mean that God has a body, goes to sleep, or gets into a state of roaring drunkenness. We understand what the passage is trying to communicate if we have seen a drunken soldier ready to take down anything in his path. Likewise, a bare-bones chronology does not develop the personality of the characters it mentions, and a personal letter may leave out details familiar to its recipient.

One famous passage used in the discussion of women's roles is the intriguing description of the ideal woman, a description that King Lemuel's mother offers to inspire her son Solomon to choose a good wife. If we take the genre into account in this passage, we quickly realize that the Proverbs 31 woman is a poetic and composite picture, written in a particular culture. Some elements will fit our culture, but others will not. Would it be accurate to interpret Proverbs 31 by teaching all Christian women to learn to spin flax or to card wool? A modern woman may have nothing to do with flax or wool (v. 13), yet still fulfill the principle of working with "willing hands" and paying attention to the physical needs of her family. Can we say that a woman's labor must be with her "hands"? Can it be with her mind or with her legs? Do we keep an oil lamp lit in our home all night because this woman's "lamp does not go out at night" (v. 18 ESV)?

Christians can become silly when interpreting the Bible. Reading a poem or a novel, they would draw principles from a passage and not become stuck on a literalism detached from the meaning of the work. I am not saying words are unimportant or that the Bible is not to be interpreted literally. The Scripture is God's Book, and every word has a divine purpose. But God chose to use humans to pen those words, which are placed in a context and written with a variety of goals in mind. Those words must be understood in the context of the work.

In the Old Testament we find books generally categorized as history, law, poetry, and prophecy. Before trying to understand what a passage means for me, I must first put it in the context in which it was written. God's word of promise to prolong Hezekiah's life by fifteen years cannot be taken out of the historic account and applied to Christians willy-nilly. If I have cancer, wake up one morning, and read that passage, I cannot conclude that I will have fifteen more years to live.[8] Unfortunately, many naive and well-meaning Christians can be disillusioned because they have never learned how *not* to read the Bible. Paying attention to genre helps us to understand the main idea that the original author wanted to get across.

Those who study the original languages of the Bible (Hebrew for the Old Testament and Greek for the New Testament, with a little Aramaic here and there) have the advantage of seeing some of the structure that escapes us in translation. They will notice parallel structures, word plays, and grammatical hints such as a quick staccato of verbs that speed up the action, words that sound similar, or an arrangement of incidents that draws attention to the central point. However, even in translation the Bible is rich for those who are willing to take the time to dig out its treasures. The more we know our Bibles the more we will see how each author structures a book, and how later Bible authors refer to the truths taught in earlier parts of Scripture.

Looking at the Progression of Scripture

Genre is not the only question. We must decide how the truths taught in one historical period apply in a later period. For example, within the books containing the law, we have very specific laws about mixing milk and meat in stews or about the kind of shovel to use in covering excrement while traveling in the desert.

How did Jesus treat these laws? How did He fulfill them? What did the apostles do with them? What place do they have in the church? Are these laws still to be applied today? Are they as important as the Ten Commandments? Why or why not? The books of the law contain moral law, family law, political law, and ceremonial law. Deciding how these laws are to be applied in the life of a twenty-first-century believer is not simple, and other principles of Bible interpretation must clarify such decisions. Highly qualified scholars have written excellent books on this subject. You will discover a wealth of new understanding of the Bible if you take the time to reflect on these issues individually and in the context of your church Bible studies.

Use the Bible to Interpret the Bible

The complexities of biblical interpretation are such that true Christians are often at odds with one another over the application of scriptural passages. Does the Bible give us overarching themes that can help us decide how to look at a passage?

We do have principles that help. The first is that we must always interpret the Bible by the Bible. We learn this lesson in Luke's account in Acts of people who lived in a town called Berea (in northern Greece) who heard the apostle Paul preach. Rather than immediately believing everything he said, they took the time to search their Old Testament Scriptures to check him out. Far from condemning their suspicion, Luke praises them. This Berean attitude is the one we must take as we search the Bible. We are not suspicious, but eager to understand. Does it fit with other passages? How? What is the relationship?

Let's take our ideal woman of Proverbs 31 again and check her against the rest of what the Bible says. She dresses in "fine linen and purple." This passage surprises us when we look at other Bible texts about women and how they are to dress. In 1 Peter 3:3–4 we read: "Your beauty should not consist of outward things like elaborate hairstyles and the wearing of gold ornaments or fine clothes; instead, it should consist of the hidden person of the heart with the imperishable quality of a gentle and quiet spirit, which is very valuable in God's eyes."

One passage implies that a woman should look as elegant as possible, while the other teaches her not to rely on dress for her identity. We bring these passages together with the help of texts such as the Song of Solomon, which rejoices in a woman's beauty and sexuality and the book of Esther. Esther's beauty was a tool in the Lord's hand to protect His people from annihilation. Other passages describe harlots who use their beauty for wicked purposes.

The New Testament passage teaches women not to *rely* on clothes for her beauty and identity. Isaiah 3:16 shows us what such arrogance produces: "The daughters of Zion are haughty and walk with out-stretched necks, glancing wantonly with their eyes, mincing along as they go, tinkling with their feet" (ESV). Women are not to use their bodies for seductive and ungodly pleasures.

But because of what we learn (and what Peter also knew) from Proverbs, we know that when Peter downplays clothing he is not saying that a woman should look frowzy or slouchy in order to prove how holy she is. Putting these passages together helps us understand the general principles about women's dress: It pleases God for women to look beautiful, but they are not to rely on such beauty for their identity, nor should they misuse it for unholy, seductive purposes. These passages are a very limited example of how one Scripture passage enriches another.

Interpreting the Bible with the Bible keeps us from going off the deep end, emphasizing one minor instruction or incident and distorting the true message of the Scriptures. Christians challenge one another in understanding the Scriptures. The amazing power of God's Word that corrects our understanding of God and His will is one of the Christian's most treasured possessions.

Looking at Jesus' Method for Interpretation

The most important principle for Bible interpretation was taught by the "ghostwriter" of the Bible, so to speak. Although each book was penned by a man, the Spirit of God was behind it all. Jesus is "the Word" personified, and He is the one who really knows how to interpret the Bible. After He rose from the dead, He surprised two depressed disciples as they walked along the road, discussing the terrible news of His death. Failing to recognize Him, they are shocked to discover that He seems to know nothing of the catastrophic news of the weekend—Jesus of Nazareth has been crucified! Jesus gently scolds them for not understanding the Scriptures. Had they read more closely, they would have understood that He had to die and be resurrected. The author, Luke, recounts what Jesus did for these fearful disciples: "Beginning with Moses and all the Prophets, He interpreted for them the things concerning Himself in all the Scriptures" (Luke 24:27).

In these short words we find the main principle for interpretation of the Bible: it is *all* about Jesus. Our task is identical to that of the disciples, to see Jesus in all the Scriptures. It is easy to see that the

New Testament is all about Jesus. The apostle Paul says that without the death and resurrection of Jesus our faith is "worthless," and we are to be "pitied more than anyone" (1 Cor. 15:17, 19). Few would object that Jesus' birth, life, death, and resurrection are the key to the New Testament. But Jesus' Bible study on the road teaches us that He is also the center of the entire Old Testament.

In addition to putting each passage into the context of its genre and its original purpose, we must also put each passage, each story, each proverb, and each commandment into the context of the grand story of history—that of Jesus Christ. We must ask of a passage, "What does this passage teach us about Jesus?" If we don't answer this question, we will never find the right moral application for our personal lives. Only as we see how a particular story increases our understanding of Jesus Christ will our vision be cleared to see what we should draw from that passage for our own use or for the use of the church.

In understanding our Proverbs 31 woman, we looked at the genre (a poetic model woman) and at other passages about women's activities.[9] But we must also understand how the beauty of Christ wraps us and covers us, making us beautiful in God's eyes, presenting us to God as a perfect, spotless bride. We have not really understood our Proverbs woman until we have understood her in her original genre, in the overall Bible story, and in her relationship to the central figure of the story—the Creator-Redeemer Jesus Christ. Only when we have seen these three aspects of a passage can we begin to make sensible application of the Bible's truths to our own lives.

As we understand what Christ has accomplished, we will see the differences between the Old Testament use of a passage and its use for us in the church. Though God's character and morals do not change, He shows us more and more of Himself as the story goes on. For those of us in the postresurrection era, the Christian faith is both simpler to understand and also more demanding. We have seen the apex of God's revelation and have the presence of the Holy Spirit to help us understand the living Word.

Understand the Cosmic Perspective

As we look at the Old and New Testaments, we realize that Jesus' coming changed many things. God's nation in the Old Testament is a picture of the kingdom in heaven, but the fulfillment of God's promises to that kingdom are broadened and apply to all nations in Christ. Jesus Himself becomes the focus of worship, rather than Jerusalem as a physical place. Jesus Himself becomes the fulfillment of each of the Ten Commandments, so that we do not have to grieve the absence of the stone tablets. Jesus Himself is the perfect King, so we are no longer to expect a king on the physical throne in Jerusalem. Jesus Himself is the perfect Judge, so we will no longer try to make theocracies on earth. Jesus Himself is the perfect Shepherd, whose church is universal, so we cannot place ultimate trust in any human shepherd of our souls.

Jesus Himself is the perfect prophet who has revealed a perfect Word, sufficient for all our needs, so we don't have to plunge into trances expecting more truth or some extraordinary personal experience of enlightenment. Jesus Himself is our perfect Priest, so we no longer need animal sacrifices and priests to escort us into the presence of God. Priests no longer give us yes and no, *urim* and *thummim*[10] answers to our questions of guidance, since Jesus gave us His Spirit to write the truth on our hearts, so that we can "prove out" the will of God. We don't ever go back to the old structures before Jesus came.

Through His Holy Spirit, Jesus is working to bring to Himself all those who have been given to Him by the Father. We are now in the calm of mercy that comes before the judgment storm.

Failure to understand this major structure dooms us to misunderstanding God's family, God's Word, and the place women play in God's story. If, on the other hand, we respect them, we begin to see a glorious picture of how women fit into God's plan for history. God does not squash women, but glorifies them by including them in His plans for a Savior.

■ ■ ■

Discussion Questions

1. Are Christians today more mature in their understanding of God than Old Testament believers?

2. Sometimes Old Testament stories don't indicate whether the characters' actions are praiseworthy. Is it possible to know? How?

3. Who is the only Bible character whose morals were perfect? Are there things Jesus did that we *shouldn't* do or things He didn't do that we *should* do?

4. Jesus explained to His disciples what the Old Testament taught about His death and resurrection. How many Old Testament passages can you find that speak directly of Jesus' death and resurrection?

5. Can you think of any passages that refer indirectly to Jesus?

6. Find New Testament authors who use Old Testament passages to argue theological points. What surprises you? (See, for example, 1 Cor. 10:1–5 or Gal. 4:21–31.)

7. Should we find parallels to the Old Testament not mentioned by New Testament authors? Why or why not?

8. What arguments are used against the Bible today that were not used in the last generation?

9. Suppose someone argued that the Bible approves of women in the military because Jael drove a tent peg through a general's temple. In light of the principles in this chapter, do you think this conclusion is justified? Why or why not?

10. Why is it dangerous for the church to study only the New Testament?

■ ■ ■

Resources

Clowney, Edmund P. *The Unfolding Mystery: Discovering Christ in the Old Testament.* Phillipsburg, N.J.: P&R, 1991.

———. *Preaching Christ in All of Scripture.* Wheaton, Ill.: Crossway, 2003.

———. *How Jesus Transforms the Ten Commandments.* Phillipsburg, N.J.: P & R, 2006.

Doriani, Dan. *Getting the Message: A Plan for Interpreting and Applying the Bible.* Phillipsburg, N.J.: P&R, 1996.

———. *Putting the Truth to Work: The Theory and Practice of Biblical Application.* Phillipsburg, N.J.: P&R, 2001.

Garlow, James and Peter Jones. *Cracking Da Vinci's Code: You've Read the Fiction, Now Read the Facts.* Colorado Springs, Colo.: Victor Books, 2004. (See chapter on the formation of the canon.)

Hendriksen, William. *Survey of the Bible.* Darlington, England: Evangelical Press, 1995.

Law, Henry. *Christ Is All: The Gospel in Genesis.* Out of print. Available at www.gracegems.org/LAW/Genesis.htm.

Longman, Tremper. *Reading the Bible with Heart and Mind.* Colorado Springs, Colo.: NavPress, 1997.

McCartney, Dan and Charles Clayton. *Let the Reader Understand: A Guide to Interpreting and Applying the Bible.* Phillipsburg, N.J.: P&R, 2002.

Robinson, O. Palmer. *The Christ of the Covenants.* Phillipsburg, N.J.: P&R, 1981.

Sproul, R. C. *Knowing Scripture.* Downers Grove, Ill.: InterVarsity, 1997.

Strom, Mark. *The Symphony of Scripture: Making Sense of the Bible's Many Themes.* Downer's Grove, Ill.: InterVarsity, 1991.

Vos, Geerhardus. *Biblical Theology.* Grand Rapids: Eerdmans, 1954.

Williams, Michael J. *The Prophet and His Message.* Phillipsburg, N.J.: P&R, 2003.

www.basicsteps.org/english/bible/step5l7.htm (part of an online basic discipleship study distributed by Campus Crusade for Christ).

www.reformed.org/bible/ (see B. B. Warfield on the canon).

Our divided nation falls in behind two lines of women—one which believes it is right to give up their lives for their children and the other that it is right for their children to give up their lives for them.

—TIM BAYLY

5

■ ■ ■ ■ ■

The Baby

AMONG THE MOVING SCENES in Peter Jackson's film adaptation of Tolkien's *The Lord of the Rings* is the stirring moment when representatives from all of Middle Earth, including King Aragorn himself, bow down to four little hobbits. Appropriately, the movie did not win any Oscars for "best actor" or "best supporting actor," because one of Tolkien's themes is that the "little guy" is just as important to the success of the quest as is the army captain or ruler. Both the little guys and the big guys are flawed. King Aragorn is fearful to step into his role. Frodo fails his final test by trying to claim the power of the ring for himself. The triumph of good is not ultimately of the characters' doing. All work together and, as the wizard Gandalf explains to Frodo, "Bilbo was *meant* to find the ring."

This is exactly how the Bible stories work. The characters are flawed, but they are a team, a team that is *meant* to accomplish its goal. The goal is to keep living in hope, in the worst of circumstances, stumbling, falling and failing, but pushing up the mountain by faith, because God has promised to bring down the black gates of hell by using our small acts of faithfulness and by sending His own hero to win the battle for us. In the face of an overwhelming enemy, "There is always hope."[1]

The women in the Old Testament cling to that notion. In spite of bleak situations, there is always hope, because God has promised to bring a Savior. Contrary to what some argue, women are everywhere in the Bible's pages. Try taking women out of the book of Judges and see what is left! Godly Old Testament women eagerly expect and long for the Messiah. For some, their deepest heart's desire is that the promised seed be born. Others have lost sight of the promises, but in God's design, they contribute to the salvation of the world by obeying what God asked the original woman to do: help Adam. Help him have children, help him subdue the earth, help him by believing God's Word, help him by fearing God rather than men, help him by carrying the promised seed. Ultimately, all of Israel's sorrows, defeats, and suffering will find their solution in that promised baby.

Old Testament women were not *only* wombs, to be used and discarded like test tubes where eggs have been fertilized. God sees the hearts of women, just as He judges the hearts of men. But women are called to obedience *as women. Women* have wombs and are called to put them to the service of the Creator, should He bless them with a husband and children. The dramatic questions that hover over the Old Testament stories are these: Can we count on the cosmic contract God made with humanity to send a Savior from the seed of the woman? Will that promised baby arrive? Who will He be? When will He come?

For all the patriarchal structures in the Old Testament (which I have no desire to deny),[2] women play a hugely important place on the stage of biblical history. It is from the womb of a woman that the Savior will come. Thus childbirth, a woman's natural desire for children and her powerful urge to protect them was placed by God in the world to assure not only the arrival and the survival of the human race in general, but of the unique seed that will rescue the human race from oblivion.

The Old Testament women fight ferociously for their right to bear and rear children. They also place themselves in danger to protect the lives of those children. By such courageous determination, they often rescue the seed from extinction, though their methods are far from perfect.

Eve: Mother of All the Living

When Eve plunges humanity into the death cycle, we expect the human race to be snuffed out immediately, for God has promised death for disobedience. But in His mercy, He allows Adam and Eve *to have children*. Thus, when the very first child is born to Eve, it is already a sign that God will hold true to His Word of promise. Adam speaks as a prophet when, after that day of horror and curse, he still names his wife "Eve, because she was the mother of all the living" (Gen. 3:20). It is in her physical and spiritual role as a woman that Eve is able to provide a savior for mankind. As she bears that first baby boy she cries out triumphantly, "I have borne a man, (by the help of) Jehovah!" Half the battle was won right then, because Eve did not die before bearing a son.[3]

God issues a curse because of sin, but the curse is on the serpent. That curse is really an act of mercy for Adam and Eve, since the punishment of the serpent means that human beings will fight back, and that one human being, the offspring of Eve, will one day conquer the serpent, crushing his head.

God pours out mercy and grace from the beginning. Salvation is for women but also through women (1 Tim. 2:15) even though it is the first woman's rebellion that shakes the universe. As Eve's womb opens, it opens the door of salvation for her, for all women after her, and for all of humankind, male or female. Through childbirth, hope returns to the world. Were it not for childbearing, there would never be a savior. Not only does God refrain from immediately condemning all women; He hands them the high privilege of participating in the creation of the one new man, the new Adam.

Sarah: Mother of Nations

And so we see God's answer to death: life. He allows children to be born and establishes a marked line of descendants through which the promise will come. One of the chosen ancestors of the promised seed is Abraham, with his wife Sarah. This stunningly beautiful girl grows up in a close-knit family. When she marries her half brother, Abraham, her father-in-law, Terah, moves the family six hundred miles from their home in southern Iraq to a town in present-day Syria. When Terah dies, God calls Abraham away from his home to an unknown destination, a land promised to him. With Sarah, his nephew Lot, and Lot's family, Abraham walks off into the unknown.

God promises Abraham that his descendants will be more than the sand of the sea and that all nations in the world will be blessed through them. But as time goes by and Abraham and Sarah get older and older, nothing happens. At the respective ages of ninety and one hundred, Sarah and Abraham are both "as good as dead," as one of the New Testament writers puts it (Rom. 4:19 NIV). King Solomon would later describe the impotence of an old man as when "the grasshopper drags himself along and desire no longer is stirred" (Eccles. 12:5 NIV).

God delights in making His promises difficult to believe! He promises way too much, so that no one but a miraculous God can possibly keep the promise. When God tells them that they will have a baby, both Sarah and Abraham laugh at the idea, and each tries to help God's project along. Abraham, who never hesitates to bargain with God, suggests that his servant Eliezer would be an acceptable heir, but God will not back down. Nothing but a true, physical son will do. Next Sarah coaxes Abraham to let her "bear" children through her Egyptian servant Hagar, a common practice in the surrounding societies. Her choice, made in fear, has disastrous consequences. No sooner is Hagar pregnant than she taunts Sarah and makes life miserable for her, bring-ing spiteful retaliation from her mistress.

When God finally fulfills His promise, and Isaac is born, Sarah is overjoyed, laughing with delight: "God has made laughter for me; everyone who hears will laugh over me. ... Who would have said to Abraham that Sarah would nurse children? Yet I have borne him a son in his old age" (Gen. 21:6–7 ESV). Isaac means "laughter," and we see that God has the last laugh. The long-awaited baby has arrived, miracu-lously, beyond belief! However, it is not long before Isaac is listening to another kind of laughter, that of mockery from Hagar's son Ishmael. The conflict between these two brothers and their descendants still af-fects our world today, since the races that descended from them (Jews and Arabs) are still at war.

Sarah and Abraham muddle through their wandering life in much the way we do. They are far from perfect. In her worst moments, Sarah shows fear, doubt, jealousy, spitefulness, and a lack of faith. Abraham, for his part, is so afraid of losing his life that he puts God's promise in great danger. He twice exposes Sarah to the risk of an adulterous relationship; first with Pharaoh in Egypt, then with Abimelech, a local king. Abraham is afraid for his life and his family line in pagan terri-tory, where he thinks the people have no respect for God. He asks Sarah to tell a half truth—that she is only his sister, thus making her fair game for a lustful king.

Whatever the genuine threat, by sending Sarah into foreign harems Abraham risks the purity of his marriage and the identity of any son Sarah might have. The second of these incidents takes place *after* God comes in person to tell Abraham that Sarah will have a child within the year (Gen. 18:10; 20:1–11). Had Abimelech slept with Sarah, who *could* then have believed her pregnant by one-hundred-year-old Abraham? The "father of the faith," as he is known, proved a mighty weakling.

God promised to bless nations through Abraham, but Abraham was not much of a blessing to Abimelech, who was punished by God, along with his whole city, until Sarah was given back to her husband.

The apostle Peter commends Sarah for her modesty and faithfulness (1 Pet. 3:6), but Peter is drawing attention not so much to Sarah as to God. Sarah was surely afraid when she was under Abimelech's or Pharaoh's power. The apostle is not underscoring her fearlessness, but her faith. She trusted God to rescue her from enemy territory. Peter thinks of Sarah and Abraham because he is writing to persecuted Christians in enemy territory, to slaves in the grip of cruel masters, and to women whose husbands have no faith and are therefore even more risky as "lords" than Abraham was for Sarah.

In Sarah's life we see the marvelous combination so often present in the women heroes of the Bible. They are willing to die for the sake of God's promise, and they throw themselves entirely on His grace. By the time she is ninety, Sarah is finally learning that God is faithful, and that He will keep His promise in spite of appearances. When she is in Abimelech's household, she is already pregnant. Surely if God has kept His promise to open her womb, He Himself will protect the baby from danger. Sure enough, God intervenes, keeps Abimelech from touching Sarah and compromising the line of the Messiah.[4]

When Sarah dies at the age of 127, Abraham buys his first piece of property in the Promised Land. Sarah's body, which brought Isaac to life, rests in the Promised Land, waiting for the resurrection that Abraham knew God could and would accomplish (Gen. 23:19). It is, in a sense, a woman who first sets down roots in the land God promised His people.

To learn from Sarah, we must put her in the context of the overall story. Like Abraham, she lived only a partial understanding of the promise. We are the privileged ones who have been given the power and wisdom of the Holy Spirit to submit in faith greater than Sarah's to situations that seem upside down and backward. We look at the ultimate upside-down victory of Jesus who dies to bring life and gives up kingdoms in order to gain the promised Kingdom. From our side of the cross, we can understand much better than Sarah that we need fear only God. As for other sources of fear—whether an abusive husband, a pagan society, constant persecution, a difficult boss, a hateful sister—we must follow Peter's advice: "Do not fear what they fear or be disturbed" (1 Pet. 3:14).

Sarah understood God's promise and longed for it. She respected her husband and the calling God had laid on him. She understood that Isaac was the one whose descendant would save his people. As we place Sarah in the context of her own story and in the larger context of Scripture, we can, by the wisdom of the Holy Spirit, see how to behave if we are tempted to fear wicked authorities: "Those who suffer according to God's will should, in doing good, entrust themselves to a faithful Creator" (1 Pet. 4:19).

The apostle Paul makes it clear to us in Galatians 4 that Sarah's story is not just about a woman's adventures in Palestine. Sarah understood the unique nature of the promised baby. There are no rivals and she must send Ishmael away. Though her treatment of Hagar seems harsh to us, and may have come from mixed human motivations, her promotion of Isaac as the son of God's promise was an indication of her fervor to protect the safety and identity of God's miracle baby. Paul argues that Ishmael was born "of the flesh" whereas Isaac was born "of the promise." He compares the two sons to two kingdoms. He compares Ishmael, the humanly planned son of slavery, to the physical Jerusalem "in Arabia." He compares Isaac, God's promised baby and the son of freedom, to the heavenly Jerusalem. Here we see how the apostle Paul uses the Old Testament to see what it teaches us about Jesus and His kingdom.

Deborah: Mother in Israel

From Sarah, the story moves on, through Isaac and Rebecca, through Jacob and his sons, through slavery in Egypt, through the desert to Sinai where Moses receives the law, and finally to the gates of the Promised Land under Joshua's leadership. The Israelites settle in their designated territories, having promised Joshua to give up their foreign gods and to love the Lord (Josh. 24:23). Within a generation, however, Joshua's victories have become grandpa's stories: the Jordan River separating to form dry ground, hornets chasing away enemies, the sun marking time for Joshua to complete a battle, city walls demolished by shouts and trumpets. Who can believe such tales?

Deborah appears in the book of Judges, which describes the moral degradation into which God's people slide when each man does what is "right in his own eyes," and there is "no king in Israel" (Judg. 21:25 ESV). As the unity of the nation dissolves, the central story breaks apart, and "bit actors" appear, some of whom are called judges. They are a diverse group, some raised up by God, some elected, some self-appointed.[5] They are often regional leaders, whose stories overlap chronologically, and their job description is not uniform. Some were administrators, some military deliverers, some semiprophets and some even tyrants.[6] They often seem oblivious to God's laws.

Samson, a Nazirite, whose vows involved never touching a dead body, digs into the carcass of a lion to eat the honey he finds there. Gideon melts down the golden earrings from the plunder of his battles to fabricate an idol, as if he had never heard of Aaron's golden calf. This careless disobedience leads to disastrous results for the Israelites.

Deborah arrives early in the book, as the fourth judge (Judg. 4:4). She lives between Bethel and Ramah, in the Bible belt of early Israel. Joshua's family inheritance is nearby, as is that of the high priest, Eleazer, and his son, Phinehas. The famous prophet Samuel's parents lived in that area, and Samuel had drawn around him a band of prophets in Ramah, near Deborah's home. The nearby town of Bethel housed the tabernacle that God's people had used while wandering in the desert, and faithful Israelites still gathered there to offer sacrifices before the high priest.

However, even into these well-protected, well-instructed safe havens, idolatry and wickedness have infiltrated. We know almost nothing about Deborah's family, her age, her background, or how she became a judge. She may well have profited from the godly instruction available from Phinehas, even if she received it by proxy. She is a "mother in Israel," a godly woman, who longs to see Jehovah's name confessed and courageously followed. Maybe, like Samuel's mother, she had given her sons into the care of the prophets. Or her husband, Lapidoth, may have been a prophet himself.[7] Perhaps she was a widow who had spent long hours helping at the tabernacle.

Deborah judges sitting under a tree, which seems odd in light of God's instructions not to worship under trees or to set up trees and poles beside an altar (a pagan practice constantly condemned by Jehovah). Deborah's palms may be the "Baal-Tamar" of a later chapter.[8] Apart from this veiled reference, there is no indication that Deborah is in any way compromised in her commitment to the Lord. The text doesn't satisfy our curiosity about this bold woman. We are simply told, in the Hebrew word order: "Now-Deborah, woman, prophetess, woman-of, Lapidoth, she, judging, Israel, at-the-time, she."

Deborah is not one of the judges mentioned as having been directly "raised up" by God, though there is no doubt that He uses her. Through her, God sends instructions and a promise to Barak, who is told to attack the enemy general, Sisera, taking an army of ten thousand men from two of the northern tribes. In spite of the promise that God Himself will go with Barak, this timid leader replies to Deborah, "If you go, I go; but if you don't go, I don't go" (see Judg. 4:8).

Barak may not here be expressing a fervor of faith, arguing as did Moses that without the presence of God, he has no desire to move out in conquest (Exod. 33:15–16). He seems to want Deborah along as a rabbit's foot. He voices no evident concern for the reputation of the Lord's name among the pagans nor any plea to God Himself. He seems to rely not on God's promise but on the physical presence of a human representative—and a woman at that. Deborah senses his fear and lack of faith and reprimands him. She tells him that although he will win the battle, the honor will go not to him but to a woman.

The victory does eventually belong to a woman. Deborah consents to ride out with Barak, whose army benefits from God's work in flooding the Kishon River, and thus turning the enemies' nine hundred iron chariots into a handicap rather than an advantage. Like Pharaoh's chariots mired in the waters of the Red Sea, Sisera's are bogged down in the muddy overflow, and the charioteers flee on foot from the battle. Sisera himself makes a dash through safe territory for home. He comes, utterly exhausted, to the tents of a man whom he trusts. There he finds the man's wife, Jael, a seemingly gracious hostess, who invites him in for a much-needed nap. Jael offers him a bowl of milk, covers him with animal skins, and waits until he is asleep. But her personal loyalty remains with God's people, not the enemy.[9] She sneaks up on the sleeping general and drives a sharp tent peg through his skull and into the ground, thus winning a resounding victory for Israel.

Deborah's story is placed in the downward spiral of Israel's disobedience. Courageous judges and kings are only human and can never fulfill the demands made of a righteous king.[10] The chaos and terror that reigns in the book of Judges teaches us that if we are to have a peaceful, fruitful existence in the home God has prepared for us, it will only be because (as Gideon said to those who wanted him to rule) "the Lord will rule over" us.

Rather than encouraging women leaders, Deborah's story underlines the fact that women were not meant to be the leaders in Israel. It is a shame to Barak that he is so reluctant to lead Israel into battle. Deborah tells him that his lack of faith means a woman will be handed the victory. In another story in Judges, Abimelech does not want to be killed by a woman, since such is a dishonor. The point of Deborah's story is that God can crush His enemies even if He has to use a woman to do it! When Jehoshaphat calls the people back to obedience, he is careful to set men of Israel in the position of just judge.[11] Deborah herself longs for "the princes to arise in Israel." That God is willing to use a woman to win His battles in the book of Judges is meant to underline the fact that we do not save ourselves. It is not by our might or power but only by God's grace that our enemies are driven out before us.

At the beginning and at the end of Judges, the people of Israel ask, "Who will go up for us?" They need a champion, against both external and internal enemies. By the time the book is over, we realize that there is no one worthy to go up. Deborah's call for a prince in Israel is not fulfilled by the Baraks of this world. The true hero is the baby who will come one day, the promised Savior, for whom Delilah's temptations will hold no power and against whom no enemy, whether physical or spiritual, can prevail.

For the moment, God waits patiently for those who are still to be rescued. But one day, the final trumpet call will sound from heaven, and God Himself will descend to judge the entire earth. Then the Deborahs and the Baraks, weak though they are, will be seen as faithful because of the sacrifice of Christ. They will be accepted into their final rest.

Abigail: Spiritual Mother

When I meet Abigail in heaven I will ask her how she coped with such a brutish husband, how she managed to get a picnic lunch for six hundred people together in time to divert disaster on her family, and how she knew David's thinking so intimately!

Abigail lives in a town called Carmel, in the mountainous sheepherding country at the eastern edge of the wilderness of Judea, where she and her husband Nabal own three thousand sheep (1 Sam. 25:2–3). Samuel the prophet has anointed David to be the future king, since God is displeased with King Saul's disobedient spirit. The transition from Saul to David is neither smooth nor immediate. David runs for his life from Saul, whose jealousy prompts him to gather an army of three thousand men to hunt for David in the Judean desert. Like modern desert outlaws, David hides in caves and holes in the ground when Saul's forces get too close. Calm and levelheaded, David refuses to take revenge even when Saul falls within his grasp.

The story of Abigail is intentionally placed in between two stunning accounts of David's grace and restraint in sparing Saul's life. He refuses to lay a hand on God's anointed king. David's reaction to Abigail's husband, Nabal, is entirely different. Here David is confronted not with God's anointed, but with a "dog."[12] Nabal is a hated petty tyrant, whose allegiance is with Saul and against David. Abigail enters the story when David sends servants to ask Nabal for hospitality on the occasion of the sheep-shearing feast. Jewish law and tradition encouraged generosity to those in need, especially during a festival. David reminds Nabal that his men have protected Nabal's shepherds and flocks from roving thieves for the entire season, but Nabal responds rudely.

"Who is this David?" he asks. "Why should I give my hard-earned food to a runaway slave?"

Gone is David's polite restraint! His response is immediate, crass, and angry. He calls down a curse on himself if he leaves alive any male in Nabal's household. David has said to Saul in the previous story, "'From evildoers come evil deeds,' so my hand will not touch you" (1 Sam. 24:13 NIV), but he now forgets all concern for righteousness.

Nabal is not God's anointed, so there is no need to hold back revenge. David is willing to slaughter Nabal and all his male relatives over a picnic lunch, though he had so gallantly sworn that no injustice would come from his hand. In a foul temper, he straps on his sword and takes four hundred men to wipe out Nabal's household. The happy festival is about to turn into a bloodbath.

Nabal and Abigail have two residences, so this intelligent, wise, lovely, articulate wife was perhaps not present when David's first messengers arrived. Nabal's servants have probably often appealed to Abigail for good sense. They are quick to find her, begging her to intervene. They are certain that trouble is coming.

Abigail wastes no time, but sends out donkeys bearing the picnic lunches David had originally requested. She provides each man with a lunch consisting of a third of a cake of pressed figs, a portion of raisins, a third of a loaf of bread, a portion of roast lamb, some wine, and a cup of roasted grain (puffed wheat?). Not enough for a week's groceries but sufficient for a picnic lunch.

Abigail risks her own life to save her family and servants. Nabal surely treats this precious wife no better than he treats his servants or David's men. He is known as a fool, a drunkard. Abigail knows the futility of attempting conversation with Nabal when he's drunk, so she acts without his knowledge but on his behalf. She is as fair and just as Nabal is ugly and mean. A less godly woman might have negotiated to let David kill only her cruel husband. What a great chance to get rid of him! After all, no one would criticize her for David's anger. One woman couldn't be expected to stand up to the mighty hero, David.

Abigail risks her life for her drunken, bad-tempered husband, and for the men in her household. However, she is motivated by an even stronger desire to see David spared from guilt and ignominy. Abigail descends from the hills to throw herself in David's path. Perhaps she has heard his oath of doom: "May God deal with me, however severely, if I don't kill every male in Nabal's house by morning" (see 1 Sam. 25:22).

"On me lay the blame," she begs David. "Pay no attention to the wicked fool, Nabal, whose name suits him. I didn't see the men you sent."

Abigail pleads passionately with David to avoid needless bloodshed. She shows her allegiance to him by calling him "master," and argues with great wit, eloquence, and theological power with David, the anointed king. She reminds him that his life and kingship are safe, because they are bound up with the living God. Her words are prophetic, as she wishes on all David's enemies (the chief of whom is Saul) the fate that awaits Nabal. She appeals to David's awareness of serving the Lord, fighting his battles with a view to achieving the place God has promised him. In the colors of faith, she paints a picture that imagines David on the throne, with a clean conscience, and no wickedness that enemies could use to reproach him. She does not want him to have the "staggering burden of needless bloodshed" on his hands, or the guilty conscience that comes from "having avenged himself" (1 Sam. 25:23–31).

How different is Abigail's counsel to that of David's men, who have tried to persuade him to take justice into his own hands. Abigail argues just the opposite. Even the life of the rebellious, hard-hearted, wicked Nabal is to be spared, if necessary at the cost of Abigail's life, so that the Lord's truly anointed king will have clean hands and a pure heart.[13]

If only Abigail's advice had lingered in David's memory long enough to prevent him from giving in to the lust that would later motivate him to steal Bathsheba, then murder her husband. Abigail's passionate wisdom and her willingness to take risks is not the scheming manipulation that other Bible figures sometimes use to accomplish God's purposes. She speaks plainly and honestly, the passion for the purity of the king burning through her humility.

David listens to her counsel and lays no hand on her. Not insensitive to her beauty, he "lifts up her head," but is struck also by her godly plea.

He thanks God for her intervention and calls off his men, who must have been glad to think "picnic" for the evening, rather than "slaughter." When Abigail informs her drunken husband the next morning of the events that have taken place the night before, his heart fails him and he "becomes like a stone." His spiritual heart is also made of stone, and, before long, God strikes him dead and he becomes "like a stone." Upon discovering Nabal's death, David is delighted. God has vindicated him and he has not sinned. He instigates an instant courtship with the lovely Abigail and marries her (1 Sam. 25:42).

Like all the godly women whom God puts in his story, Abigail advances the cause of the promise when she is willing to pay with her life to protect the glory of the Lord's anointed. She does not become an ancestor of the promised baby, but she eagerly protects David from sin, which shows how dedicated she is to the purity of that line. She knows that David is God's anointed king and longs for the king to maintain his righteousness. Her example of godly passion is astounding. Here is a woman who has learned to serve the Lord with a pure heart in the worst of situations. She rides above her own suffering and puts God's purposes first in her life. She is a marvelous example of practicality, godliness, theological wisdom, literary finesse, affection, humility, and beauty. She lives all this as a simple wife and mother in Israel, under the control of a brutish and cruel husband.

Conclusion

We have looked briefly at four women who play a huge role in bringing the seed of God's promise into the world and in protecting that seed, both physically and spiritually. They do not accomplish this miraculous feat by becoming generals and kings. They are wives and mothers. Eve, mother of all the living and the first woman, on whom the hope of the world rests, brings Seth into the world after the agony of Cain and Abel. Sarah faithfully trusts God and her husband until

God keeps His promise and gives them Isaac. Deborah arises, a mother in Israel, when times are bleak. She longs and prays for the princes of Israel to fill their godly leadership roles and obeys all God asks her to do, encouraging Barak to "go up" against the enemy. Abigail respects her husband even though he is a drunken bully. Her heart is filled with desire for holiness, and she cares more for the honor of the name of God than for her own well-being.

God uses and honors these women as they fulfill their womanly calling to aid their men in filling and subduing the earth. God's call to battle for women is the call to serve the kingdom by serving their husbands, their families, and their homes. In fulfilling this calling, they bring about salvation and take their place of honor. When the battle is finally over, women, like the hobbits, will find that their contributions were not so unimportant, not so unnoticed as they might have thought! King Jesus will draw attention before the throng of believers to their unsung acts, and will give them the kiss of His peace.

■ ■ ■

Discussion Questions

1. God uses weak people to accomplish His goals. In what way were each of the women mentioned in this chapter weak (Eve, Sarah, Deborah, and Abigail)?

2. What were their fears?

3. How did their faith in God make them strong?

4. Was Jesus a weak or a strong hero? Explain your answer.

5. Read 1 Samuel 25 carefully. To what does Abigail appeal in arguing with David? What is her main concern? What parallels do you see between the three stories in chapters 24, 25, and 26? What is different? Why does the author put these three stories together?

6. What can we tell about the motivation of Eve, Sarah, Deborah, and Abigail? Support your answers from the Bible.

7. What dangers threatened the promised baby in each story? How was the seed protected? By whom?

8. What hints of the promised baby can you find in the book of Judges?

9. How does the Lord vindicate each woman in this chapter?

10. What can you rightly deduce for your own life from these stories? (Be careful to respect the principles mentioned in the last chapter.)

Resources

Clowney, Edmund P. *The Glory of the Coming Lord: Discovering Christ in the Old Testament.* www.graceonlinelibrary.org/theology/full .asp?ID=413.

Davis, Ralph Dale. *Such a Great Salvation: Expositions of the Book of Judges.* Ann Arbor, Mich.: Baker, 1990.

Dyrness, William. *Themes in Old Testament Theology.* Downers Grove, Ill.: InterVarsity, 1979.

Fokkelman, J. P. *Reading Biblical Narrative: An Introductory Guide.* Leiderdorp: Leo Publishing, 1999.

Fortner, Donald. *Discovering Christ in Genesis.* Darlington, England: Evangelical Press, 2002.

Gaffin, Richard B., Jr., ed. *Redemptive History and Biblical Interpretation: Shorter Writings of Geerhardus Vos.* Phillipsburg, N.J.: P&R, 1980.

Hunt, Susan. *Heirs of the Covenant: Leaving a Legacy of Truth for the Next Generation.* Wheaton, Ill.: Crossway, 1998.

Longman, Tremper and Ray Dillard. *An Introduction to the Old Testament.* Grand Rapids: Zondervan, 1994.

Murray, John. *Redemption, Accomplished and Applied.* Grand Rapids: Eerdmans, 1961.

Warfield, B. B. *The Plan of Salvation.* Grand Rapids: Eerdmans, 1984.

Wood, Leon. *Distressing Days of the Judges.* Grand Rapids: Zondervan, 1975.

Zuck, Roy B., Eugene H. Merrill, Darrell L. Bock, eds. *A Biblical Theology of the Old Testament.* Chicago: Moody Press, 1991.

I will plant her for myself in the land; I will show my love to the one
I called "Not my loved one." I will say to those called "Not my people,"
"You are my people"; and they will say, "You are my God."

—THE PROPHET HOSEA
(HOS. 2:23 NIV)

6

■ ■ ■ ■ ■

Odd Ancestors

WHEN I WAS OLD ENOUGH to dare, I would sneak down on
Christmas eve after everyone was asleep, to stare at the pile of presents
under the tree. I stood shivering in my p.j.'s, mesmerized by the blink-
ing lights. I never dared touch any for fear they would either melt away
like a dream or attack me. My creative brother was known to make
"self-opening" presents—or worse! Finally, I would tiptoe up the sides
of the steps, snuggle back into bed, and fall asleep imagining the crinkle
of my Christmas stocking at the foot of my bed.

I am not the only little girl to have stood in the shadows, waiting
for Christmas. As we arrive at the first chapters of the New Testament,
we see four grown-up girls who are mentioned in Jesus' family line.
These women, sinners like me, stared into the dark mists of the future
and caught a glimpse of the only real Christmas the world would ever
need. They waited in the dark and the cold, but the Christmas star did
not appear in their lifetime.

These four women had much in common. What brings them together in the first chapter of the first book of the New Testament is, first of all, that they all bore children who would be ancestors of Jesus. The entire Bible story is built around the created family structures God made when He put Adam and Eve together and asked them to fill the earth. The Old Testament stories move from generation to generation, following the line of the promised Savior. The human family tree begins with the very first man Adam and his wife Eve, to whom huge promises are made for the future. Then sin plunges them into darkness, and the lights go out for a long, cold Christmas eve. But God preserves the family line and protects it so that the promised seed, a longed-for child of Eve, one day appears and the light of Christmas morning finally comes. The world is not doomed, as in C. S. Lewis's *The Lion, the Witch and the Wardrobe,* to a world of perpetual winter without Christmas.

In the last chapter, we saw God keeping His promise through Eve, Sarah, Deborah, and Abigail. They were faithful wives and mothers, though they could not see the promise clearly. All four, however, lived, married, and had children within the community of God's people, the Jews. As we move into the New Testament, we get a surprise that will prepare us for the explosive mystery of the gospel: God's work of salvation will soon be going global. Our first hint of this in the New Testament texts is actually the reference to four *Old Testament* women who were waiting for Christmas.

Tamar: A Canaanite Bride

Tamar is the first woman mentioned by Matthew in the ancestral line of Jesus. She lives before the law has been written down, before the Ten Commandments are given, before God delivers His people from Egypt. Her relationship with Judah, Joseph's older brother, is sandwiched between the account of Joseph's kidnapping and his honorable disengagement from the seductive wife of Potiphar. After Joseph is sold into slavery, Judah moves away from his brothers and settles down near a non-Jewish friend in another town. There he sees a beautiful Canaanite woman named Bathshua and marries her. Er is their first son, and Judah chooses Tamar as a wife for him. Probably both Er and Tamar live in Judah's home. God cut Er's life short, however, because of some terrible wickedness which the text does not reveal.

Since Judah married a Canaanite woman and lived in pagan territory, we don't know whether he bothered to instruct his family about God's nature and promises. Whether or not Tamar is familiar with the promises God has made to Jacob, she longs for children. When Er dies, Judah instructs his second son, Onan, to do his brotherly duty. Judah follows a culturally accepted practice, called levirate marriage, that will later become Israelite law. If a man died childless, his brother was to marry the widow. The first male born would carry the name of the dead brother. Subsequent children would carry the name of the living husband.

Onan participates willingly enough in the first part of his duties—enjoying Tamar's sexual favors. But he deliberately sabotages the plan to produce descendants for Er by "spilling his seed" on the ground (Gen. 38:9–10). Like many young men, Onan sees sex as pleasure to be seized, not as godly love to be offered. "Spilling his seed on the ground" is not only a selfish act performed in secret; it is an affront to God Himself. Onan cares nothing for the seed God has set apart as holy. His secret act is punished openly, however, and he joins his brother in the grave.

By this time, Judah is regretting his choice of Tamar for a daughter-in-law. He thinks she is bad luck. He sends her back home to her father, stringing her along with a promise that he has no intention of keeping: she must wait for his youngest son Shelah to grow up. Tamar is bound by betrothal to Judah's household but evicted from it. We don't know how many years she waits, but eventually, it becomes obvious to her that Judah has no intention of honoring his duty to provide her with a husband and descendants.

So Tamar takes things into her own hands. When Judah's wife dies, Tamar disguises herself as a cult prostitute (common to the pagan religions of the day) and sits beside the road where Judah will pass, on his way to the annual sheepshearing. She correctly assumes that Judah's lust will get the better of him. He invites her aside, contracts to pay her a young goat in exchange for her sexual services, then offers his wallet and photo ID, so to speak, as collateral—his staff, belt, and signet ring.[1]

When Tamar becomes pregnant from her encounter with Judah, the neighbors make sure Judah finds out. Unaware that he himself is the father, Judah condemns her to be burned. Judah is probably glad to get rid of this bad-luck daughter-in-law. But as the town authorities drag Tamar out to be burned, she triumphantly produces Judah's staff, belt, and signet ring. "These belong to the man whose child I carry!" she announces. For all his wickedness and weakness, Judah admits to the act, declaring of Tamar, "She is more righteous than I!" Tamar bears twin sons, and one of them, Perez, becomes the ancestor of David, and eventually of Jesus (Gen. 38:24–30).

Why is such a seedy story placed so deliberately, so proudly into the lineage of Jesus? Tamar is one ancestor you would not include in your creative memories album! This story shows us how silly and dangerous it is to draw direct moral application from a Bible character's behavior. Though Tamar's faith is praised, she is not placed in the biblical text to encourage barren women to seduce their fathers-in-law! However, like scores of other Old Testament women, Tamar clings to her rightful desire for children. Barren women all over the world, and women in societies where forced abortion has torn their babies from their wombs against their will—these women understand the intensity of Tamar's desire.

A man who knows God's promises and should have kept his word to Tamar has stolen away *her* "birthright"—her right to bear a child.

She has waited long enough. Soon she will be too old for children. At the risk of her reputation and even her life, she forces Judah to keep his promise. Several other women take huge risks and cry out, "Let the blame be upon me!"[2] Tamar doesn't say it in so many words, but she doesn't care about the public humiliation her actions will cause. She knows the shameful nature of the family into which she has come, yet she is determined to move forward.

Tamar's sin is real. Had she known more of the God of Israel, perhaps she would have waited on God and not taken things into her own hands. This honored ancestor of the Christmas baby was a sinful, pagan woman who seduced her father-in-law. Her desires were honorable, and her defenders were nowhere to be found. In His grace, God forgives the sin of both Tamar and Judah, and wraps them into the family line.

Rahab: A Canaanite Prostitute

On the next page of Matthew's family album we find a woman called Rahab (which means "proud"), who lived about six generations after Tamar, in a home built into the wall of the city of Jericho. From the window of her home in the wall, Rahab could gaze out over the surrounding countryside in the fertile regions near the Jordan River. Rahab was a prostitute familiar to the city officials. No doubt in the weeks preceding the story in which she first appears, new clients from outside the city walls had arrived, full of tales about the legendary army massed across the Jordan River. This army walks across rivers and receives food from the skies. They find water in rocks and wear clothes that never deteriorate. On the eastern shores of the Jordan River, they have already defeated two nations who refused to make peace with them.[3] They may soon be headed toward the city. Jericho is astir, and scores of frightened people are coming inside the city walls for protection.

One night, two men arrive who are not interested in Rahab's physical favors. They need another kind of help. They are enemy spies, on the run. She has a quick decision to make: remain faithful to her own town and denounce the spies, or cover for them in the hopes that they will spare her life when they arrive for battle. This decision calls for faith, one way or the other. Either Rahab believes her own city impregnable (in which case she denounces the spies), or she believes the Israelites will be the victors (in which case she protects the spies).

Rahab has already given thought to the reason for this army's success: "As soon as we heard it, our hearts melted . . . for the LORD . . . is God in the heavens above and on the earth beneath" (Josh. 2:11 ESV). Rahab takes the plunge. She hides the men under flax stalks that are drying on her roof. When the police arrive, she tells them to hurry. They can still catch the spies if they go straight out the front gate. Having dispensed with immediate danger, Rahab strikes an agreement with Joshua's men: I've saved your lives, now you save mine and those of my family.

The spies promise to save anyone in her house when the Israelites come to fight. She is to mark her home by hanging a red cord from the window. Rahab shows them where to lie low, in the western hills, on the opposite side of the city from the Jordan River. After three days, when the hunt has been abandoned, the spies cross the Jordan River and make their way back to the Israelite camp. When God brings judgment on Jericho, Rahab and her family are rescued.

Rahab could have wandered off after the battle to live in prostitution again. Her arrangement with the spies had not included a promise to become a part of God's people, but they find a place for her and her family "outside the camp." We find out later that Rahab adopts the name of God and, with her family, throws in her lot with the Israelites. She becomes a member of a people "set apart" by God. In Rahab's case, we have the rare summary conclusion of a New Testament author: "By faith Rahab the prostitute received the spies in peace and didn't perish with those who disobeyed" (Heb. 11:31).[4]

Rahab marries a man from the tribe of Judah called Salmon. They settle down and have children and grandchildren, one of whom is a man named Boaz, who probably carried a certain stigma as the descendant of a prostitute, and a pagan at that.[5] Rahab rejoices in the God who has rescued her from her life of sin, her worship of pagan gods, and her deserved destruction. Imagine how amazed and grateful she must have felt all her life that the two men "just happened" to slip into her home for protection. In fact, she was the one who needed protection, and she got it.

Eager to learn of God, Rahab may have learned and taught to her children and grandchildren Moses' words about God's law: "What other nation is so great as to have their gods near them the way the LORD our God is near us whenever we pray to him? . . . do not forget the things your eyes have seen or let them slip from your heart as long as you live. Teach them to your children and to their children after them" (Deut. 4:7–9 NIV).

That Boaz took God's mercy to heart is evident in his attitude toward our next pagan woman. We are beginning to see a pattern.

Ruth: A Moabite Daughter-in-Law

You are probably more familiar with the story of Ruth than with that of Tamar or Rahab. Ruth was from a tribe that descended from Moab, Lot's son by an incestuous encounter with one of his daughters. After the destruction of Sodom and the death of their mother, Lot's two daughters live with their father in the desolate hill country. The girls find their singleness too great a burden and have no faith that God will provide marriage partners for them among the caves. So on consecutive nights, they each get Lot drunk, sleep with him and get pregnant. The older daughter has a son, Moab, and the younger a son, Ben-Ammi (Gen. 19:36–38). The nations that descend from these two boys become the Moabites and the Ammonites.

God protects these nations for some time, but their sins eventually become so great that God's punishment falls on them. One particular incident at a place called Peor particularly angers God. A Moabite king, Balak, hires a famous prophet, Balaam, from a faraway town (a known center of pagan worship) to curse the Israelites. But Balaam doesn't even earn his travel expenses, let alone his honorarium. Try as he might, he can only utter blessings. So Balaam and Balak cook up another scheme. They send in the women warriors—Moabite women to seduce the Israelite men, enticing them to worship the idol Baal at a place called Peor (Num. 25:1–5). This sin is so blatant and detestable, that it is remembered for the rest of Israel's history. God makes a law barring any Moabite from becoming a part of the people of God for ten generations after the incident at Peor.

But, true to His merciful nature, God turns this curse into a blessing for one Moabite woman, who is so eager to belong to Jehovah that she refuses to stay in her homeland when her Israelite husband dies. By faith, she turns her back on all she knows, and on any hope of remarrying in her own culture. She stubbornly (and lovingly) follows Naomi, her Jewish mother-in-law, back to Bethlehem. Ruth knows that as a Moabitess, she will not receive a warm welcome in Israel. She probably has little hope of remarriage or children. She will have to live down a "Bourbon Street" reputation as a seductive idol worshiper, even though she as an individual proves herself gracious, generous, faithful, and kind. However, like the other women in this chapter, Ruth is willing to abandon her reputation and her people because she is desperate to belong to God's people. Here we see a woman who, in her heart, has understood what the true family of God is—the family of faith. She concentrates on God, who has great plans for her and honors her sacrificial love.

Naomi and Ruth arrive in Bethlehem with nothing except Naomi's self-pity and bitterness. Ruth becomes a day laborer, joining the ranks of the poor who, in Israelite law, had the right to pick up leftover grain after the harvesters have finished in a field. "As it happens," Ruth finds herself in the field of an older man named Boaz, who immediately notices the beautiful young foreigner (Ruth 2:1–5).

Here we see what Boaz has learned by being the son (or at least descendant) of the foreign prostitute, Rahab. Though he realizes that Ruth is a Moabitess, he does not turn her away. Boaz instructs his workers to leave extra grain for Ruth and tells her to keep gleaning in his fields, where she will receive protection. When Naomi finds out who has shown such kindness to Ruth, she is delighted, for she knows Boaz to be a relative able to act as a "kinsman-redeemer."

This practice is similar to levirate marriage. A close relative could buy out the property of a dead man and marry his widow, thus raising up a descendant for him and rescuing his name from oblivion. In Boaz's case, one relative is in line ahead of him. If that man does not want to exercise his right, Boaz can purchase Naomi's land (from her dead husband and sons), and at the same time "inherit" the widow, Ruth.

Naomi perhaps senses that Boaz is hesitant to propose to Ruth, since he is much older and extremely respectful of the young woman. Naomi suggests a risky course of action to Ruth. She has no reputation to save, however, for her status as Moabitess makes her already disreputable in the minds of the Israelites. Following Naomi's explicit and puzzling instructions, Ruth wears her most beautiful clothes and her best perfume, then sneaks down after dark to the threshing floor where Boaz and his men have been working. There she waits until Boaz is asleep, then slips under his covers (Ruth 3:1–8). Naomi could not have instructed Ruth to give a more direct signal that she was available. In fact, her behavior seemed to reinforce her reputation as a Moabite prostitute.

But Boaz acts honorably, unlike Judah's behavior with Tamar. He protects Ruth's reputation and does not respond sexually. He reads

Ruth's heart and asks her to be patient until he can make a legal proposal to purchase her dead husband's land, and to receive with that inheritance a treasure he never believed could be his—a loving wife, young and beautiful, whose heart is full of love for him and for his God.

Ruth Bears the Kinsman-Redeemer

Ruth's dubious, though undeserved, reputation is alluded to by Boaz's well-wishers when he concludes the legal necessities to buy the property and inherit Ruth as his wife. They cannot help bringing up Tamar's history. Perhaps they think that Boaz has already ceded to the foreign temptress. Whatever they think about Boaz and Ruth or about Tamar and Judah, it is fascinating to see that Tamar is not forgotten, but lives on in Jewish history. Nor is the womanly work of Rachel and Leah forgotten. In spite of their jealousies and pettiness, these squabbling sisters are lauded because they "together built up the house of Israel" (Ruth 4:11 ESV).

The references to women like Tamar, Rachel, Leah, Naomi, and Ruth are common in God's story of the Savior. Women, as we have seen, are crucial to the gospel story *because* of their place as wives and mothers, not in spite of it. Women contribute to the strength of their nation and to the establishment of the heavenly nation of believers by "building up the house of Israel"—bearing and rearing children, loving their husbands, and admonishing their fellow believers with the truth of God's law.

Ruth, the pagan Moabitess becomes the mother of a son, Obed, who is identified at the end of the story as the "kinsman-redeemer" (Ruth 4:18–22). Boaz is no longer the focal point of male godliness at the end of the book of Ruth, though he is a stunning example of a godly man. His tenderhearted thoughtfulness and grace; his respect for women, servants, and foreigners; his selflessness; his industry; his sense of responsibility; his attention to detail in his work; his willingness to get to the heart of things rather than hiding behind stereotypes. But Boaz doesn't seek glory.

At the end of Ruth, all eyes are turned to the baby in Naomi's lap. Naomi's women friends say to her, "Praise be to the LORD, who this day has not left you without a kinsman-redeemer. May he become famous throughout Israel! He will renew your life and sustain you in your old age" (Ruth 4:14–15 NIV). It is not Boaz who is the focus of attention as the kinsman-redeemer, but the baby. It is only the baby who will lie on Mary's lap who can truly renew our life and sustain us in our old age. It is not Boaz, and it is not Ruth's son Obed who will renew life and sustain us or who will, as the elders put it, "be famous in Bethlehem" (Ruth 4:11 NIV).

Can you see Ruth and Naomi, standing in the shadows of church history, catching just a glimmer of the light of the world in the bright eyes of Obed as he lies on Naomi's lap? Obed will father Jesse, who will in turn father David, a man after God's own heart, and a picture of the King to come. But it is David's descendant, Jesus, who shines the full light of the world on to Ruth's hopes.

Bathsheba (Bath-shua): Wife of a Hero

The last peculiar woman to appear in Jesus' genealogy is the "wife of Uriah," whose name was Bathsheba. Bathsheba had a number of ties to King David. She was married to Uriah, the Hittite, one of David's thirty famous "mighty men." Because her husband was a Hittite, many scholars assume that she was a foreigner. That the other three women mentioned in Matthew's genealogies are also foreigners lends weight to this assumption. Bathsheba's name is given at least in one place in its Canaanite version (Bath-shua) (see 1 Chron. 3:5 KJV).

While David is running from Saul, he gathers around him a brave but frightening "Robin Hood" band of disgruntled men from a variety of backgrounds and nationalities. Among these courageous warriors are Bathsheba's husband, Uriah, and her father, Eliam. Bathsheba's grandfather is Ahithophel, one of David's wisest and most trusted counselors. Eventually, Ahithophel will betray David by going over to the rebel king Absalom's camp. This heart change may be motivated in part by his disgust at David's actions toward his granddaughter. Ironically, it is Ahithophel who advises Absalom to cement his authority over David's kingdom by raping in broad daylight the ten concubines David leaves to look after his palace when he flees for his life from his rebel son Absalom.

Consensual Sex?

David's relationship with Bathsheba is completely out of line. The Bible does not state explicitly that Bathsheba is a willing partner to David's lust. The king does send men to take her, so some scholars argue that she is an unwilling party. However, Bathsheba knows David's weakness for women (who didn't?). She knows that the king is, exceptionally, not off to battle that weekend. She knows that her home is in full view of the palace roof. My husband is amused that I so systematically pull the curtains across our bedroom window. He tries to persuade me that no one can possibly see into our third floor window, surrounded as it is by trees. But I just want to be sure! Bathsheba pulls no curtains across. In addition, she makes no attempt, as did Abigail, to dissuade David from sullying his reputation as king (1 Sam. 25:32–34; 2 Sam. 11:2–4). Abigail argues brilliantly and passionately, at the risk of her life, to stop the king from doing evil. Bathsheba says nothing and complies with David's advances.

Whatever Bathsheba's attitude, David is clearly in sin. He does not catch an accidental glimpse of Bathsheba and turn his heart from sin. He does not content himself with a longing gaze, an act of adultery in itself, as Jesus would later say. David not only lusts in his heart; he puts his lust into action, and Bathsheba becomes pregnant. David tries to cover his sin by inviting Bathsheba's husband Uriah back from the battlefield, assuming the tired soldier will spend the weekend across the street, at home with his wife. No one would then need to know that Uriah is not the father of the child to be born.

But Uriah refuses to sleep with his wife, since David's soldiers were always celibate when on duty. The first night he is in town, Uriah lies like a faithful puppy on the doorstep of the palace, honoring his soldier's vows and not returning to his home. The second night, David tries, without luck, to loosen Uriah up with wine. After two nights, David gives up and sends his friend back to the front lines with a sealed death warrant in hand—an order to be handed to the commanding officer to put Uriah in a battle position where he is sure to be killed! Little did Uriah suspect that his beloved king and battle companion had charged him with carrying his own death warrant. The commander obeys and sends Uriah close up to the walls of the enemy city, where he and others lose their lives (2 Sam. 11:14–17).

It is little wonder that David's relationship with Bathsheba falls under God's judgment and their first baby dies. But David is heartbroken when he understands the extent of his sin. God pardons David's callous treachery and Bathsheba's apparently willing adultery, blessing their son, Solomon, who becomes the heir to David's throne.

Ancestral lines in the Jewish culture did not include women. In Matthew's genealogy no less than four women are mentioned. At least three, and probably all four are foreigners. Apparently God did not appreciate the famous prayer some Jewish men used to pray, "Thank you God for not making me a Gentile, a woman, or a slave." All four women in the Matthew genealogy had irregular marital relationships. Not one is condemned in the Scripture. On the contrary, they are paraded in honor before all Christians to this day, because they all contributed to bringing the Savior into the world.

Into the New Covenant

Why does God include such dubious characters in the line of the Savior? Are we beginning to get the picture? These women are among the first hints that God's grace will explode, pouring out on the nations, opening the floodgates to rich and poor, slave and free, male and female. Already the Old Testament had many examples of foreigners who receive an inheritance with the nation of Israel, but when we get to the birth of Jesus and to His message in the Gospels, we begin to see more clearly how God's promise is accomplished. God does not turn His back on women, but honors them as they seek His name and rely on His strength to bear children. When the Savior arrives, He is the fulfillment of the promise given to Eve so long before.

Christianity does not squash women. It honors them in their femaleness and hands them the great privilege of becoming a part of God's family through the Savior whom they bring into the world. Obviously, it is not only women who truly understand the gospel. Feminine nature is not, by definition, more divine. This book is by a woman, for women, and about women, so I am concentrating on the woman's place in the cosmic contract with the universe. The Old Testament story includes many stories about evil men and how they, too, are forgiven and made a part of the covenant in spite of their estrangement from God's laws and will.

However, it is the thesis of this book that women are not squashed by the Christian faith. They are, on the contrary, given a place of high honor in the Bible, not only in the New Testament but also in the Old Testament. They play a huge part in the accomplishment of God's will and in the arrival of the promised seed. It will not surprise us as we move now into the New Covenant to see Jesus relating to women with honor, affection, tenderness, and compassion. Jesus loved Eve, Tamar, Sarah, Rahab, Ruth, Abigail, Bathsheba, and scores of other Old Testament women.

Now we will examine His love for His mother, for His women supporters, and for the sisters who will come into the kingdom when the gospel goes to the ends of the world. It is only Jesus' love, the love of the only perfect, holy man that can teach us who women truly are. He understands and loves us best. God made women in His image, and Jesus Christ will recreate them in His own image, as He redeems them and renews them.

■ ■ ■

Discussion Questions

1. Read the stories of Tamar (Gen. 38), Rahab (Josh. 2; 6; see also Ps. 87:4 and Heb. 11:31), Ruth (the book of Ruth) and Bathsheba (2 Sam. 11; 12; Ps. 51). What do they have in common? How are they different?

2. How might Jesus have used these stories to tell His disciples "all the things concerning Himself"?

3. Compare Joseph's behavior in Genesis 37 and 39 with Judah's in Genesis 38. How does each value his reputation? How does Joseph's cloak serve? Judah's ring, staff, and bracelets?

4. What becomes of Tamar and her children?

5. Why is it so important for foreign women to be included in Jesus' ancestry?

6. What nationalities become a part of God's people? Can the church be identified with one nationality?

7. What do these four women teach us about our attitude toward foreigners, prostitutes, immigrants, and political enemies?

8. Can we know who is in God's family? If so, how? If not, why not?

■ ■ ■

Resources

Clarkson, Sally. *The Ministry of Motherhood: Following Christ's Example in Reaching the Hearts of Our Children.* Colorado Springs, Colo.: WaterBrook Press, 2004.

———. *The Mission of Motherhood: Touching Your Child's Heart for Eternity.* Colorado Springs, Colo.: WaterBrook Press, 2003.

Cundall, Arthur E. and Leon Morris. *Judges, Ruth: Tyndale Old Testament Commentaries.* D. J. Wiseman, gen. ed. London: Tyndale, 1968.

DeWaard and Nida. *A Translator's Handbook on the Book of Ruth.* United Bible Society, 1973.

Fortner, Donald. *Discovering Christ in the Book of Ruth.* Darlington, England: Evangelical Press, n.d.

Hunt, Susan. *Your Home: A Place of Grace.* Wheaton, Ill.: Crossway, 2000.

Kaiser, Walter C., Jr. *Mission in the Old Testament: Israel As a Light to the Nations.* Ann Arbor, Mich.: Baker, 2000.

How, except by the virgin birth, could our Savior have lived a complete human life from the mother's womb, and yet have been from the very beginning no product of what had gone before, but a supernatural Person come into the world from the outside to redeem the sinful race?

—J. GRESHAM MACHEN

7

The Baby's Mothers

AMONG OUR FAMILY MEMENTOS are the discharge papers of a direct ancestor of my husband, a certain William P. Moore, an eighteen-year-old Englishman from the Isle of Mann who enlisted in the U.S. Navy on August 26, 1863. He was just over five feet tall. William served as a mercenary on a Union ship transporting slaves from the South to freedom in the North. As he listened to the slaves in the hold of the boat singing praise to God, he became a Christian. My husband would probably not be a Christian today had young Billy not had the crazy idea of enlisting in the U.S. Navy. He returned to England, where he married and had descendants, raised as Christians.

In heaven, I want to spend as long as it takes to hear the stories of the believers in my family line. Then I'll listen to the stories of your family, of a fifth-century Christian from China or a nineteenth-century believer from Nigeria or, possibly, a twenty-fifth-century

Christian from Peru. God's love for families is proven by the individuals whose names are recorded in His Word.

The genealogy of Jesus in Matthew holds a pivotal place in God's story, since it introduces the first chapter of the first book of the new contract between God and His people. The entire Old Testament hangs on "generations": "These are the generations of" . . . Moses, Abraham, Jacob, and so forth. Finally, the eagerly awaited baby arrives. But the genealogy of Jesus in Matthew and Luke brings us to the beginning of a new humanity. As Eve was the mother of the living, Mary will be the mother of the first man to bring new life.

Mary

The four foreign women we discussed in the last chapter are included in Jesus' genealogy for excellent reasons.

First, they show that non-Jews (Gentiles) were incorporated into Jesus' line in the Old Testament. The great "mystery of the gospel" to which Paul often refers is that the good news of salvation marches out beyond the walls of Jerusalem. Flickering hints of this message are abundant in the Old Testament, and it shines through Jesus' ancestral list in Matthew 1. The light of the world will shine not only in Jerusalem, but will penetrate all the shadowy corners of the world.

Second, the female ancestors show that God's promise is not just to men but to women. God favors women with His love and blessing. Jesus had many mothers, and would have many sisters (Matt. 12:46–50; see discussion in chap. 8). He had women ancestors and would have (by faith) women descendants.

Third, their presence gives a boost to Mary's reputation, which will be put in question when she bears Jesus. The best Mary and Joseph can hope for is a little compassion for their supposed impatience. Some surmise that Jesus eats with "sinners" because He fits the role, His birth obviously being the fruit of fornication.

Mary Accepts Her Call in Faith

Mary, a quiet and godly teen, is terrified by an angel with an incredible message. When the angel tells Mary she is to have a child, she replies, "How will this be, since I am a virgin?" (Luke 1:34 ESV). Her question is not full of doubt, as was Zechariah's when an angel tells him that his elderly wife will bring John the Baptist into the world. Mary puzzles over the logistics of the arrangement, rather than questioning the angel's word.

Mary will bear the stigma of "unwed mother" for the rest of her life. Jesus was "the son (as was supposed) of Joseph" (Luke 3:23 ESV). The neighbors' tongues wag, since she becomes pregnant before marriage. Who will believe she is pregnant by the Holy Spirit? Mary probably shares the truth with her sister,[1] and her elderly relative, Elizabeth knows. Joseph, her fiancé, believes the unlikely news only when an angel appears to him. Later, Jesus' whole family suffers from mockery: "'How did this wisdom and these miracles come to Him? Isn't this the carpenter's son? Isn't His mother called Mary?' . . . And they were offended by Him" (Matt. 13:54–57).

Mary does not benefit socially from Jesus' birth, history, and ministry. Even her other children think Jesus is crazy and try to sow doubts in Mary's mind. We cannot imagine the pain and isolation Mary goes through. As the prophet Simeon tells her, "A sword will pierce your own soul" (Luke 2:35). Mary is lonely in her reflections. Joseph probably dies early, and she is obliged to keep much to herself. But Mary also speaks volumes when she takes her place in the story that began in the Garden of Eden. For Mary is a woman, and she is the mother of Jesus Christ.

We realized as we looked at Old Testament women that they are not in the stories chiefly for moral lessons, but because God uses them to play both a physical and a spiritual role in accomplishing His promise to bring the Savior into the world. The baby that Mary bears is unique. If we needed any proof beyond the creation story that women are fully in the image of God, we surely have it in Mary. For the irony of the Matthew genealogy is that it ends with Joseph! We've examined the women in Jesus' line, but that line ends abruptly. Joseph did not contribute his physical seed to the conception of the promised child. Biologically and humanly speaking, only Mary is Jesus' parent.

Consider the incarnate Christ. He is human because He was "born of a woman," as the apostle Paul puts it (Gal. 4:4). In this sense He derives His created, human, "image of God" nature uniquely from Mary. At the birth of Christ, the Holy Spirit hovers in an act of new creation to produce the first new man, the first of many brothers, the progenitor of a redeemed people. So Jesus' bodily humanity comes through Mary and His messianic claim comes partially through the marriage bond, so that He is truly the son of David.

The Bible proves to us over and over again that Jesus had to become like us. Paul emphasizes that Jesus Christ was born of a woman (Gal. 4:4–5). Hebrews says that those who need saving and the one who does the saving are "brothers" and "have one origin" (Heb. 2:11 ESV). Jesus, the baby who is the Savior, is known as the "second Adam," because He is born in a physical body and He will die in order to present believers "faultless" before God (Col. 1:21–22).

Jesus' humanity comes only through Mary. We need look no farther to see how highly God has honored women. After Eve's scandalous sin, God blesses her with the promise that from the womb of the very one who dragged the human race into degradation and shame would come a descendant who would save her and all of God's children from the clutches of the tempter. Women are not derivative images, second-class citizens, or diminished humans. God sets apart to His ends the womb of a woman and allows her human genetic makeup to determine the human nature of the God-Man, Jesus.

Here, finally, Eve's hopes and dreams come true. Cain was not the promised one, nor was Abel, nor even Seth. Eve must have realized, as time went by, that none of her own children would prove to be the promised Savior. Generations of women would bear and bury children before that Savior would be born. Nevertheless, Eve, Sarah, Rebecca, Tamar, Rahab, Ruth, Bathsheba, and countless other women exercised faith, brought children into the world, and set their hearts on the Savior to come. They looked through the shadows to the star of Israel who would appear.

Does this mean that Jesus was bequeathed with Saviorlike qualities *because* He was born of a woman? Was Eve the true heroine, listening to the true counselor, Satan? Is Adam the weak fool and God the Creator a wicked demi-god, as a heretical group called the Gnostics taught?[2] Certain feminist theologians raise woman-ness to godliness. The feminine is ultimately closest to divinity. The hero of the fast-moving *Da Vinci Code* is not so much one of its characters as the "divine feminine," a principle of spirituality that depends not on a physical savior who died and rose, but on a ritual sex orgy.

The New Testament makes no moves in this direction in its treatment of either Jesus or Mary. Jesus inherited flesh from His birth mother and from all the humans who contributed to her birth, all the way back to Adam. But each of these individuals was sinful. Mary does not become a sinless icon who contributes to Jesus' perfection. Because Jesus was born of Mary, He was fully human, fully "image of God." But because Jesus was born of Mary, He was also born into a body under the curse of sin. The apostle Paul says that Jesus was "made . . . sin" for us (2 Cor. 5:21). Jesus becomes sin not only on the cross, but by taking on a body of sinful flesh. Jesus does not derive perfection from Mary. On the contrary, it is Mary who must derive perfection from Jesus, by faith in His death and resurrection. She, more directly than Naomi, will be sustained by the baby on her knees, who is the Kinsman-Redeemer.

Jesus, Son of Mary, Son of God

For Jesus is not the son of Mary only. He is also the Son of God. Were He not fathered through the power of the Holy Spirit, He would be no Savior at all. The initiation of this seed, the fathering of this child, cannot come through any human father, whose seed is dead within him. God does what Judah's son Onan refused to do. He provides a living seed for the spiritually dead husband. Jesus' birth is the result of a cosmic levirate marriage. Joseph's seed is dead in sin. It died with Adam. It died with Abraham. It died with David. It died every time a son was born of sinful flesh, for that son could never claim eternal life, nor could his name live forever. Once the first Adam fell into sin, his progeny could never produce a holy seed able to provide salvation. None of Adam and Eve's ordinary descendants could ever lay claim to the eternal throne.

The ancestry of Jesus traced through Joseph in Luke and in Matthew[3] arrives at a dead end, for Joseph had *nothing to do with* the conception of Jesus Christ. God Himself steps in to provide a son for Adam's family and to rescue the name of the human race. Just as Boaz assured the line of Ruth's husband, so Jesus guarantees Adam's family name and line. God Himself serves as the levirate husband to humankind. Through His intervention, Mary bears a holy son who carries Adam's name and purifies it by uniting it to the name of God Himself.

To pick up another image from the Old Testament, Jesus is the "younger brother" of Adam, as it were, the one upon which God sets His love. Old Testament stories are full of younger brothers who end up ruling over their older brothers. Joseph is the prime example. He dreams of his brothers and parents bowing down to him. Jesus is the younger brother of Adam who saves the human race from obliteration. It is this younger brother who will rule over His parents and His brothers and sisters. In fact, before Jesus, every knee in heaven and on earth will one day bow.

The Old Testament stories of miraculous births prepare us for the stable, where we see the most surprising birth of all. Jesus is born to a virgin. Mary's virginity is symbolic of the purity of the human line. God does all the purifying and resurrects the sons of Abraham from extinction. "[Abraham] considered not his own body now dead, when he was about an hundred years old, neither yet the deadness of Sara's womb" (Rom. 4:19 KJV; Heb. 11:12). Tamar's line was tainted. Rahab's line needed cleansing, and Bathsheba could offer nothing pure. Eve would look in vain to her own sons to fulfill the promise. Even Jesus, who came to bear our sins, must be transformed by His death and resurrection, to be reborn as the first new man, a life-giving Spirit (1 Cor. 15:45).

Son of David through Joseph

So what do we make of Joseph? Is he irrelevant to God's project? No, Joseph has his place in the Savior's line. By hanging Jesus' identity on the line of Joseph, the Bible shows the value that God places on covenant marriage. God fulfills His promise in a unique, miraculous combination of the designated Old Testament representative, patriarchal structures (so maligned by feminists) and the physical, created structures of childbearing. It is interesting that the woman's obedience in bearing Christ, and the man's obedience in being the head of his home through the marriage relationship both play a crucial role in the birth of our Savior, and in His validation as Messiah. Jesus is born to a betrothed Mary. Already, legally, Mary's child will be taken on by Joseph, since Joseph does not break the betrothal. In the social structure, Jesus will legally be the son of Joseph the carpenter from Nazareth. Joseph and Mary register their citizenship in Joseph's town.

Joseph's covenant marriage relationship to the mother of Jesus is enough to prove the Savior's right to an identity as the Messiah. Of course, there is an irony here. You will accuse me of wanting to have my cake and eat it too. Either Jesus can or can't claim messianic identity through Joseph. If Joseph had nothing to do with the birth, if his seed is dead, and if he is descended from Jeconiah (on whom a direct curse was placed in relation to the throne of David),[4] then how does his lineage prove that Jesus is the Messiah? On the other hand, if it does prove Jesus' line, then why does he have nothing to do with Jesus' birth?

The answer lies in the mystery and in the irony of the Incarnation. It shows how God miraculously restores the structures that withered away by sin. Neither Mary nor Joseph can produce a sinless Savior. God must do it all. God comes down and becomes a baby. But He chooses the womb of a woman and the lineage of a man, thus renewing and resurrecting His created structures by breathing into them the breath of life who is the very Word that spoke the world and its order into existence.

Son and Brother of Christian Women

Jesus shows us the important relationship we twenty-first-century women can have with Him. Was it important that Mary bore Him? Did she have a special claim on His life because she was His mother? Mary has a special place of honor in all of human history. Here I am, thousands of years after the birth of Christ, speaking of her, admiring her humble faith, but most of all affirming the grace of God in choosing her as mother of the Savior. She would rejoice with us only insofar as we are looking at Christ. This was her source of joy when she went to her cousin Elizabeth's' house: "From now on all generations will call me blessed, because the Mighty One has done great things for me, and His name is holy" (Luke 1:48–49).

Mary's place in the kingdom, however honorable, hangs on her relationship to Jesus by faith in His death and resurrection. We will discuss in the next chapter how important it is for Mary to understand this truth and how Jesus goes about gently teaching it to her.

Shady Women of the Present: Mothers of Jesus

Mary's mothering of Christ brings us all a miraculous message from heaven. If you are in Christ by faith, *you* are Christ's mother. Whether you are single or married, childless or a grandmother, if you have become a part of God's family by the exercise of faith in the Savior who came into the world to save sinners, then you, a sinful woman, are Christ's sister. You are His mother. Mary, with all the privilege she had, is no more privileged than you. You have just as intimate a loving relationship with the Lord Jesus Christ as His own mother.

Never Too Shady for the Light of the World

You may be a woman with a "past" like Rahab or Bathsheba. You stand in the shadows, shivering, afraid to approach the light of the Christmas star; afraid to touch the present Jesus offers you. You are reaching to touch the robe of Jesus, to be healed, but you are petrified that He may turn His gaze on you. Perhaps you have given your body over to sexual sin in the past or are even now mastered by sexual lust, by greed, by selfishness, or by any other cruel and devilish master. You may have deliberately wandered from the path you knew would lead to true happiness, and now you think it is impossible to come back.

If Rahab the prostitute could be counted in Jesus' line, as one of His famous ancestors, you can be one of His famous descendants. It is to you that He says, "Behold my sister. Behold my mother." There is not one woman reading this book who could confess to a sin so great that Jesus would not be willing and able to forgive it. The only sin that cannot be forgiven is the sin that will harden your heart more and more. If every time you hear an invitation to grace, you turn your back, unwilling to receive forgiveness and perfection from the hand of your Savior in exchange for the filth you will give Him, then you will eventually become unpardonable. So lay down your pride. Write your story beside that of Tamar, and have done with your life of misery and loneliness.

Perhaps you have given in to fear or to the pressure of those around you and have aborted your own baby. So, in a way, did David. Take heart. There is forgiveness. Perhaps you have abandoned your husband in act or in thought. The prophet Hosea brought his wandering wife back over and over to show how great is God's mercy. Perhaps you have been unwilling to name the name of Christ in your workplace. Peter, the powerful apostle, once denied that he ever knew Christ, after having spent years in His personal company, absorbing His love. There is hope for you. If God could make Peter into a bold preacher of the gospel, He can use your mouth to sing His praises in the office.

Out of Shadow, Light

You not only receive salvation; you can also bring others to receive it. The woman at the well had five husbands and was a mess morally. But the living water she received from Jesus overflowed from her mouth and life until an entire village was listening to the good news. God doesn't despise the mouth that bit into the fruit of disobedience. He purified it to pour out fruitful words of praise to His name. From the mouth of the king's mother in Proverbs proceed words of wisdom and her children rise to call her blessed. Even if you have cursed God, as Peter did, you can still sing God's praises.

Never Had a Shady Past?

If God has spared you from a dubious past and you have grown up never remembering a day when you didn't know God as your Father and Christ as your Lord, you will have other temptations. You will tend to harden your heart to those whose sinful behavior so shocks you that your anger becomes not a reflection of God's righteousness, but of your own pride. The women cited among Jesus' ancestors are not the "holy" women, but the outcasts. Your churchgoing habits will not delight God if your heart is hard. God has forgiven you for trusting in your own righteousness, just as He forgave Tamar and Rahab for indulging in illicit sexual relations. You and Rahab must share that same longing to be a part of the family of God by faith. God only requires humility of heart and our simple acceptance of His love. It is Jesus who raises up our line and keeps our name safe.

Don't be surprised when things look upside down. All of the women in Jesus' line had upside-down situations. Mary never expected to be known as a fornicator. Rahab never expected to live with the conquerors of her people. Bathsheba never expected to live in the palace, and under such circumstances! Tamar never expected to have a child with Judah. Ruth never expected to live in the territory of Judah and to become an ancestor of Christ. It all looked upside down. When you look at your life in the light of the Incarnation, perhaps the angel on your Christmas tree is dangling upside down. You're looking, but you can't find the presents. You wake up, but there is no crinkle at the bottom of the bed.

Your upside-down life is in the hands of a loving Father. God is a lion who tears you, but He is also the one who heals you (Lam. 3:10). He will lead you through the dark days to see His light once again.

Be Christ's Mother

You can be proud to be a woman. Jesus entered the world through the womb of a woman. If you're married, and can't get up enough courage to have a baby, don't be afraid. Do not listen to the world's reasoning that you have to have enough money, a bigger home, a better car, more job security. God made you to bear children, and it is His longing that we keep up the Christmas tradition.

The virgins reading this book will not be having babies in the next few months. Mary's experience was a unique shattering of the created order, when God broke in and began a new creation in the person of the Second Adam, by taking on human flesh Himself. But God wants you to continue loving the order that still reigns. Fill your womanliness with humility, compassion, courage, and the power of the Spirit.

To those who are not married, or to whom God has not given children though you may have longed for them: Do not despair. You are still Christ's mother. Jesus told you so. You must believe Him and exercise your womanly gifts and compassion to those around you. When you minister to the least of His children, you are ministering to Him. Your circumstances cannot stop you from exercising the privilege of being Christ's mother. You are His mother, you are His sister if you do the will of the Father. You must not give in to despair.

Risk Your Reputation

If you have become a member of Christ's family line by faith, then you are one of Jesus' sisters, one of His mothers, and you will bear the disgrace of Mary. You will be seen as odd and your reputation may become questionable to the rest of the world. Mary's innocence and honor did not gain her acceptance from those around her. She and her son were derided, pitied, scoffed. When you step into the light of the gospel, you step out of the shadows of the world, into God's glorious light. But don't expect your friends to understand you.

When my daughter-in-law Christina was four and one-half months pregnant with her first child, she and my son Julien discovered that their baby, Jonathan, would not live when he was born because his skull and brain were not forming correctly. But the desperation of this news never made them consider ending his life in the womb just because the doctors presumed he would die at birth. They carried him to term and cried with delight at his birth, though the tears were also of mourning for his death, which occurred only nine hours later. But in mothering Jonathan, in bearing him, receiving him, giving her love and compassion to him, Christina was exercising the reality of mothering Christ.

She gave her love to the "least" of Jesus' brothers, and He received it from her with gratitude and joy.

Your decision to follow Christ will make you a peculiar woman in the eyes of the world. A few of Christina's acquaintances couldn't understand why she didn't just have an abortion, if the baby was going to die anyway. (Do we kill our children today because they will die one day, anyway?) Our culture teaches us that we women control the destiny of our children. Christina and Julien allowed God to determine the times of Jonathan's life.

If we Christian women follow our Savior through the dark, cold times, we will, for eternity, stand in the blazing warmth and radiance of Jesus, the morning star, whom we will see in all His glory one day, when we step out of the shadows of this world into His presence. Until then, we have a chance to shine like stars in the universe, bearing the light of the gospel to those who still stand shivering in the cold, hoping to catch a glimpse of the Savior. Mothers of Jesus, let's be fruitful in bringing many sons and daughters to the glory of the resurrected Christ.

■ ■ ■

Discussion Questions

1. How does the fact that Mary carried and bore Jesus prove that women are fully in God's image?

2. How are Mary and Eve alike? How are they different?

3. What part do women play in the coming of the Messiah?

4. Why didn't God create another human being from the earth in order to get a pure Savior?

5. Why is Joseph important in Jesus' family line?

6. Who does Jesus say is His mother?

7. If you are a Christian woman, how have you been misunderstood by non-Christian friends or coworkers?

8. As a woman, how are you tempted to define yourself by the world's standards instead of by God's standards?

9. What does it mean for you to think of yourself as Jesus' mother or sister?

10. If you are single or childless, are you still Jesus' mother? Why? Why not? How can you experience this sense, if you have not had children yourself?

■ ■ ■

Resources

Machen, J. Gresham. *The Virgin Birth of Christ.* Ann Arbor, Mich.: Baker, 1965.

Gaffin, Richard, ed. *Redemptive History and Biblical Interpretation.* Ann Arbor, Mich.: Baker, 1981.

Robertson, A. T. *The Mother of Jesus: Her Problems and Her Glory.* New York: George H. Duran Co., 1925.

Smart, A. Moody. *The Three Marys.* Edinburgh: Banner of Truth (originally published 1862), 1984.

Tripp, Ted. *Shepherding a Child's Heart.* Wapwallopen, Pa.: Shepherd Press, 1995.

[Jesus] was traveling from one town and village to another, preaching and telling the good news of the kingdom of God. The Twelve were with Him, and also some women who had been healed of evil spirits and sicknesses: Mary, called Magdalene (seven demons had come out of her); Joanna the wife of Chuza, Herod's steward; Susanna; and many others [women] who were supporting them from their possessions.

—LUKE 8:1–3

8

■■■■■

Jesus and Women

MY DAUGHTER TESSA kept me waiting long after her due date on July 12. In fact, my mother-in-law missed the birth by two days because she returned to England in time for Princess Diana's wedding. Tessa arrived on July 30. I shouldn't have been surprised when, years later, I had to change my flight home from London because Tessa's first baby also was late. Miranda had kept her parents waiting from April 9 to April 25. When she finally burst into their lives, she was all the more joyously greeted. Her father, Oliver, was so taken with her that he made a few mistakes at his last music rehearsal, eliciting from one of the female musicians, "Ah, he's dreaming of Miranda!"

The tender joy of this little family is only a glimpse of the joy God's family receives when *the* baby arrives. The world waited for generations to see this unique child, whose birth was planned before the world began. Throughout the history of God's people in the Old Testament, women longed for children, but especially for *the* baby, the promised Savior. They sacrificed their own needs and comforts, hoping for the son who would deliver them from suffering and sin.

When Jesus arrived, was He all that women hoped for? Was the world's Christmas baby worth the wait? What would His coming mean for women? How does the promised Savior treat women?

Jesus Respects Women

Jesus' treatment of women is not only a perfect example of loving and respectful attitudes toward women; it is a subtle programmatic statement of who women are. The Gospels recount at least twenty-two incidents of Jesus relating personally to women of varying ages, races, and situations. Jesus also refers in His teaching to the daily activities of women, such as bread baking, shopping, housecleaning, pregnancy and breast-feeding. Jesus does not mistreat or ignore women. As a child, He had the godly influence of Mary, whose song of praise to God, recorded for us in the Bible, shows the depth of her understanding of the Old Testament. He may also have had contact with his elderly relative Elizabeth and her husband, Zechariah. The prophetess Anna's prediction of Jesus' calling may have echoed in Jesus' ears as His mother repeated it to Him. As an adult, He was willing to go against many societal expectations to show how much He loves women and is worthy of their confidence. They respect Him because He respects them so much.

The Gospel writers do not waste time on the romantic details of Joseph and Mary's courtship or sensational scenes of the Samaritan woman's adulteries. However, their straightforward stories graphically show us the respect Jesus holds for women.

Respect for a Prostitute

Jesus even respects disreputable women. One such woman bursts in on a banquet in Simon the Pharisee's home. Infamous for her immorality, she brazenly approaches Jesus, who is reclining at table as an honored guest. In her hands, she carries a fancy alabaster jar full of scented oil. Overcome with love for Jesus, she begins crying, kissing his feet, and anointing them with the oil (Mark 14:3). The tears and oil make quite a mess, so she unpins her hair and begins wiping up the oil. The scene causes a stir, confirming the guests' worst suspicions about the woman and creating new suspicions about Jesus. Only prostitutes let their hair down in public. To the guests, this woman's behavior must have seemed seductive.

What could Jesus do? Draw up His feet and scold her for her sins? Apologize to His host, and ask the woman to leave? Take her aside for a lesson in manners? Ask Simon to throw her out? What would your pastor do?

Finally, Simon can stand it no longer. Just how far will the great prophet Jesus let this woman go? Admittedly, Jesus has done much good, healing thousands and performing astonishing miracles, but if He is a prophet, He must know what kind of woman she is and Old Testament law: "You shall not bring the fee of a prostitute . . . into the house of the LORD your God in payment for any vow" (Deut. 23:18 ESV). How can Jesus accept a committed act of worship from this sinful woman?

Jesus respects the woman's outburst of love for what it is: the gratitude of a heart made new, a life restored, a soul washed clean by the forgiveness and healing power of the Son of God. He knowingly receives her wages *in payment of a vow*—her vow to love and serve Him with all she is and has. "Her sins have been forgiven, for she has loved much," declares Jesus, while chiding Simon for failing to offer Him the most common of expected courtesies. "Your faith has saved you," Jesus says to the woman. "Go in peace" (see Luke 7:50). What loving care Jesus shows this outcast! How happy she must be as she returns home in the freedom of forgiveness.

Most of the time, when Jesus heals and forgives, He restores people to their own families and homes. This woman, however, may be one of the few who had no such ties and was therefore free to follow Jesus and His disciples to Judea, to support them from her own financial means. She, or women like her, may be part of the fulfillment of an Old Testament promise: "She will . . . prostitute herself . . . her merchandise and her wages will be holy to the LORD. It will not be stored or hoarded, but her merchandise will supply abundant food and fine clothing for those who dwell before the LORD" (Isa. 23:17–18 ESV).

Respect for Mary of Bethany

Jesus shows respect for Mary, Martha's sister, when she, too, pours expensive perfume on Him (John 12:3). Jesus defends her "wasteful" action to the protesting disciples. Mary understands that Jesus is marching off to His death, so she is preparing His body for the tomb, perhaps fearing that she will have no access to the body when He dies. She has thought about the implications of Jesus' teaching. If Jesus can command her brother Lazarus back to life, He is the master of life and death. Yet He still says He must die, so His death is inevitable.

Jesus defends Mary to the critical disciples. He makes no derogatory comments about her, no jokes about women's extravagant emotions. He refuses to criticize her for her "financial waste" and makes no cracks about women's spending habits. What is Jesus' summary of her behavior? "Wherever this gospel is proclaimed in the whole world, what this woman has done will also be told in memory of her" (Matt. 26:13).

General Respect for Women

Jesus never slanders or belittles women. He does not make generalizations about them. He does not shut them out of conversations or ignore them. He doesn't make them feel small or relegate them to an inferior status. Everything He says and does in relation to women shows the utmost care and respect. He speaks to them in public without embarrassment and invites them to talk with Him. He looks them in the eye and deals with the reality of their situation and often sets them up as shining examples of faith and godliness. It is obvious by the way Jesus treats women that He would not favor the repressive practices that some recommend to "keep women in their place." This is not Christ's attitude toward women. If Jesus the Christ does not squash women, then Christianity should not squash them either. Jesus teaches us how to honor women.

This book is for women, but any men who have had the patience to read this far may glean some wisdom from Jesus' attitude toward women. It is easy for men to stop listening when a woman speaks, or to think of her input as less important, tainted by illogical emotion. Jesus here values not only Mary's thoughtful evaluation of the necessity of the cross and resurrection, but also the emotion that Mary pours into her act of devotion.

One of my daughters graduated from a high-ranking liberal women's college and decided to pursue theological study in a seminary where 90 percent of the students were men. After a few days in her new school, this *summa cum laude* graduate came home bemused. "Mom," she said. "It's a little hard to get used to. Whenever I enter the conversation, the guys stop listening!" Jesus does not stop listening when women speak.

Jesus Honors Women

Jesus Honors a Woman's Womb

The first honor the Son of God accords women is to choose a womb as His first home. This sounds strange, because who chooses his mother? No one, except Jesus, the Creator of the world. He created Mary and chose to honor His Father's desire to rescue humanity. God did not rescue humanity by creating a new man out of the earth, as He had made the first man. God chose instead to honor His promise to Eve. By entering His creation through the door of a woman's uterus, He makes good His promise to Eve that one of her descendants will crush the Serpent's head. This descendant will be the world's first new man. So in His first earthbound "act" (His Incarnation and birth as a baby) Jesus honors women. God would not live in the temple David wanted to build, and Solomon asked, "Will God indeed dwell on the earth? Behold, heaven and the highest heaven cannot contain you; how much less this house that I have built!" (1 Kings 8:27 ESV). God does come to "dwell on earth" as Immanuel, and his first home is the glorious temple of a woman's body.

Jesus Honors Women as Mothers and Sisters

He also honors them by calling them "mothers" and "sisters." He considers believing women to be a part of His intimate family. There are no secret, privileged circles, requiring special status or mystical knowledge. You don't even become a part of Jesus' family by belonging to His genetic line. Jesus does not destroy physical families but intentionally downplays His blood relationships, since believers enter his spiritual family and are united to Him in love through faith. Places in *this* family are not earned by bloodline, wealth, gender, or by any other kind of status but are bestowed by God on all who believe: "To those who believed in his name, he gave the right to become children of God—children born not of natural descent, nor of human decision or a husband's will, but born of God" (John 1:12–13 NIV). Jesus can bring forth children like this because He *was* a child like this, born not of natural descent, nor of human decision or a husband's will, but born of God.

Jesus Honors Women by Seeking Their Worship

Another way Jesus honors women is by seeking them out to minister to them. It is Jesus who initiates contact with the Samaritan woman at the well, placing Himself in a compromising situation, asking this adulterous woman for a drink of water. Wells are the setting for many a romantic encounter in Old Testament history. Little does this woman know that she will find a very different kind of "husband" at the well. Like Abraham's servant seeking a bride for Isaac, Jesus has surely been praying for this woman before she arrives. In her encounter with Him, she finds true faith and becomes a part of Christ's body, His bride.

Jesus initiates encounters with women hesitant to approach Him. He stops to interact with a woman who touches Him in a crowd and is healed of internal hemorrhage (Mark 5:30–34). He seeks out Mary to speak with her privately and individually after the death of Lazarus, when she doesn't know what to say (John 11:28–32). Jesus meets directly, personally, and intimately with women to teach them and lead them in their faith.

Jesus Honors Women by Protecting Them from Lust

When Jesus reprimands males for their lust, he shows how deeply He honors women (Matt. 5:28). He places the blame not on the seductivity of women (though He would not hesitate to confront a woman about this issue), but on the heart motivations of men. Any man who so much as looks at a woman in lust has already, in principle, committed adultery. Jesus implies that it is a man's job so to protect the honor of a woman that he will refuse to allow himself to lust after her. According to Jesus, even divorce is only necessary because of the hardness of the male heart: "Moses permitted you to divorce your wives because of the hardness of your hearts. But it was not like that from the beginning" (Matt. 19:8).[1]

Jesus Honors Women by Commissioning Them as Witnesses

One of the highest honors Jesus gives women is to commission them as the first eyewitnesses of His resurrection. His mother

Mary is the first witness of His birth, and Mary Magdalene is the first witness of His new birth (John 20:17–18). He charges women to inform the disciples that His body is no longer in the tomb and that they are to meet Him in Galilee (Matt. 28:8–10). Though women were not legal witnesses in Jewish society, their testimony carries weight in Christ's kingdom. It is no compromise to the credibility of the gospel that women carried the good news to Jesus' apostles. Jesus takes delight in the believing hearts of the women who come to His tomb in heart-wrenching hope, in illogical faith, in tender, passionate love for Him. They lingered at the cross until the last, and now they are the first to watch by the tomb. As the first witnesses, it is their word against that of the Roman and Jewish authorities. Guess whose word counts with the Judge of the universe!

Jesus Teaches Women

He Meets Their Intellectual Needs

Jesus doesn't sit under a fig tree writing vague poetry about women. He meets their needs by stimulating their minds and teaching them theology. No rabbi of the day bothered with women, but Jesus includes them in His teaching, much of which occurs in casual home situations or outside in the fields. Mary of Bethany (Luke 10:40–42), though possibly exceptional in her hunger for theological understanding, was not the only woman to sit and learn from Jesus. Women assume a surprising intimacy with Him. They have enough close personal contact to feel comfortable coming at almost anytime, to ask Him whatever they have on their minds, and when they come, Jesus teaches.

Mary Magdalene (the woman who boldly crashes the party at Simon's home), Mary the mother of James and Joses, Salome, and others follow Jesus and care for His needs. In their daily contact with Him and with the male disciples, these women receive instruction, along with wisdom, love, and friendship. Some women are overly bold, like the mother of James and John, who, like a good Jewish mother, requests the best seats in heaven for her "boys" (Matt. 20:20–21).

Direct theological discussions are recorded between Jesus and the woman at the well (John 4:7–26) and between Jesus and the sisters, Mary and Martha of Bethany (Luke 10:40–42). Among the women, these sisters seem to have had the most regular contact with Jesus and the apostles. They absorb Jesus' teaching as He spends many happy hours in their home. The Gospel accounts tell us that after teaching in the temple, Jesus spends the night on "the Mount of Olives," perhaps not under the stars, but in Bethany, on the eastern slopes of the Mount of Olives.[2]

We get a picture of the home—discussions in one room, meals in another; Martha busy in the kitchen while Mary has become "distracted" by Jesus' teaching and, perhaps plate in hand, sits mesmerized. Mary has become in our minds the typical example of the "theologian" type, but all the women in Jesus' life learn theology in their daily interactions with Him. What is theology if not sitting at Jesus' feet, then rising to serve Him in the place where He has set us?

He Meets Their Spiritual and Emotional Needs

Jesus offers formal teaching in the temple and pays particular attention to the formation of the twelve apostles. He also teaches the crowds and interacts with the Pharisees. However, His teaching goes far beyond such formal occasions. He works His truth into the hearts of women, meeting their deep spiritual and emotional needs. He senses their sins, feels their fears, and knows their desires. Jesus takes interest in the details of their personal lives. He is moved with compassion and heals a woman who is so bent she cannot stand straight (Luke 13:10–17). He notices the poor widow and as Lord of the temple, receives her offering of two small coins, knowing they are all she owns (Mark 12:41–44). He looks with tenderness into the tear-stained eyes of Martha and Mary, weeping with them and their friends at the death of Lazarus and roaring with anguish himself as He confronts death to raise Lazarus from the dead (John 11:17–37).

Jesus does not use emotion to manipulate, but He shares the pains and joys of the women He loves. He never confronts these women in anger, but gently speaks to them, using the trials of life to increase their faith in Him. Daily life becomes an occasion for spiritual lessons. He uses Martha's doubts to probe her faith. "I am the resurrection and the life," He tells her. "Whoever believes in me, though he die, yet shall he live, and everyone who lives and believes in me shall never die. Do you believe this?" (John 11:25–26 ESV).

Martha knows that her dead brother's body is in the tomb and that Jesus could have healed him. Her anguished response is still a confession: "I believe that you are the Christ!" she says boldly, ignoring the threat of the Jewish authorities to put anyone out of the synagogue who confesses Jesus as the Christ (John 9:22). Martha is among the few who clearly confess that Jesus is the Christ. Most call Him a blasphemer or ask, "*Could* this be the Christ?"[3] Mary and Martha have met the Lord spiritually, and they believe.

When Jesus heals, He also deals with spiritual and emotional needs. He will not allow the woman with the issue of blood to sneak off in the crowd once she has touched His robe. He wants her to know who has healed her and what she really needs—forgiveness of her sins (Matt. 9:22). As Jesus instructs the woman at the well, He teaches her, but He also focuses on her pain and loneliness to show her her spiritual need for living water (John 4:7–26). In His dealings with women, Jesus reconstructs the mind, changes the heart, and engages the emotions.

Jesus Treats Women Tenderly

Jesus shows tender care for women. He is perfectly pure, never offending them sexually, but He appreciates their emotional suffering and

their physical hardships. He calls the woman with an internal hemorrhage "daughter," tenderly acknowledging the agony of her suffering.
He tells her, "Go in peace and be free from your affliction" (Mark 5:34).
Jesus uses a word related to "scourging." As this woman lays hold on
Him, and He heals her, Jesus is already taking on Himself her "scourge."
What courage she must take from Jesus, who deals with her spiritual
scourge as well as her physical ailment. For twelve years, she has been
unclean, not allowed into the temple. By His "stripes" she is accepted,
whole and forgiven in the eyes of the most holy man who ever lived.

When Jesus raises a little girl from the dead, He takes her hand and
gently draws her from the bed, reminding her family, who are paralyzed
by joy, to give her a meal (Luke 8:54–56). When Mary Magdalene is
overwhelmed with grief, the resurrected Jesus quietly speaks her name,
knowing that the sound of His voice, so precious to her, will prove His
identity (John 20:16). Even Jesus' parables acknowledge the everyday
concerns of women. He says of the crisis days of persecution, "Woe to
pregnant women and nursing mothers" (Matt. 24:19). Jesus tells many
believable stories about women—for example, the poor woman who
calls all her neighbors in to celebrate when she finds a lost and precious
coin (Luke 15:8–10).

This story always reminds me of Simone, a dear peasant lady who
was our neighbor in a small village in the south of France. One day she
was working in her tidy vegetable garden when I heard a loud shriek.
Before long, she appeared at my door, puffing in excitement, a shining
smile on her face. "C'est un miracle! Le bon Dieu m'a fait un miracle!"
she cried. The "good Lord's" miracle was the discovery, at the root of a
tomato plant, of her wedding band, which had disappeared three years
earlier. It is Simone's shriek of joy, the contagious need to share her delight, that characterizes the woman who finds her coin. Jesus tells this
story and many like it because He is acutely aware of the daily concerns
of the women He meets.

Jesus Accepts Help from Women

Financial Help

Jesus, who treats women so tenderly, is not above receiving their help. Luke tells us that while Jesus is traveling around the towns of Galilee, in the north of Israel, He and the twelve apostles are served (the word used comes from *diakonos,* from which we get our word "deacon") by Mary Magdalene, Joanna (wife of Herod's steward), a woman named Susanna, and *many other [women].*[4]

It is difficult to imagine the practicalities of their travel. Did they use a central home, big enough to bed down and feed thirteen men and "many" women? Did they divide into smaller groups, hosted by friends and relatives? Did the women pay for hotel accommodations? Arrangements are complex enough to require a treasurer who is tempted by the sums involved. Jesus' disciples make arrangements for feeding people, for the Passover meal, and for a meeting place during Jesus' death and His resurrection. Women play an integral, supportive role in such arrangements. A group of faithful women participate financially in meeting the Savior's needs while He is on the road teaching and preaching.

Physical Needs

Jesus also receives the personal ministry of women, their physical and emotional help. He receives the hospitality of Martha and Mary as they cook and entertain Jesus and His disciples (Luke 10:38–42). Jesus accepts the service of Peter's mother-in-law immediately after He heals her from a high fever (Mark 1:29–31). Jesus asks a Samaritan woman for water (John 4:7) and receives the tears of a prostitute who weeps passionately out of love for Him (Luke 7:44). He receives the anointing for His death that Mary of Bethany offers Him (John 12:2–8).

C. S. Lewis, in the *Lion, the Witch and the Wardrobe* probably had such women in mind when he writes of the comfort Susan and Lucy bring to the lion Aslan as he approaches the stone table where he must be sacrificed at the hands of the White Witch. The frightened girls walk along silently beside the huge lion, their hands grasping his warm mane. (I can never read that part of the story without crying.) So is Jesus comforted by Mary's tears over His coming death. He also receives Mary Magdalene's tears of joy when she realizes that her wildest dreams have come true—Jesus is really alive again, after three days in the grave (John 20:13–16).

Jesus Is Honest with Women

Jesus' tenderness to women is not patronizing. He doesn't wink at the apostles and "put up with" the women because their meals are indispensable. On the contrary, He really listens to them and also confronts them with their need, their sin, their lack of faith, and their hypocrisy. With the woman at the well, He is blunt enough to provoke a true understanding of guilt, without which she cannot receive the living water He offers her. He doesn't pander to her minority but states clearly that salvation is of the Jews.

When the mother of James and John begs preferential treatment for her sons, Jesus reproves her openly. "You don't know what you're asking!" He tells her and her two sons, who had probably put her up to it. "Are you able to drink the cup that I am about to drink?" (Matt. 20:22).

When Martha begins to fret and become judgmental of her sister's perceived laziness and is caught up in the importance of her kitchen tasks, Jesus reprimands her, reminding her to get her mind off the little things and on to the important things (Luke 10:40–42). Jesus goes to the heart of the matter, asking women probing questions and giving them definitive answers.

However, in His directness, Jesus takes into account that women are often in difficult social situations. He speaks to them in the context of their everyday lives, accepting their service of God in their roles as wives, mothers, poor widows, or wealthy, independent women. He doesn't hurl the biting accusations at women that He hurls at the Pharisees.

Jesus Breaks Social Stigmas for Women

Jesus' attitude toward certain social structures draws attention to the radical nature of His message and person. He sits alone with a Samaritan adulteress and spends two days in her village (John 4:40), receiving worship from her and her former lovers (possibly the most chaotic worship service ever held). He teaches women publicly and allows them to travel with Him and His disciples. He accepts the "wages of a prostitute" as a holy offering to anoint the perfect lamb for His death. He touches the dead body of a widow's son, being carried out for burial (Luke 7:11–17), apparently defying the Mosaic Law that instructed priests not to defile themselves by touching a dead body, unless the body is that of a close family member.

Though Jesus is not a priest in the formal sense, He claims a position even higher than priest. Here is the law God gave Moses for priests: "No one shall make himself unclean for the dead among his people, except for his closest relatives, his mother, his father, his son, his daughter, his brother, or his virgin sister (who is near to him because she has had no husband; for her he may make himself unclean). He shall not make himself unclean as a husband among his people and so profane himself" (Lev. 21:1–4 ESV).

In touching the dead body of the widow's son and of Jairus's daughter, Jesus is saying that He considers these dead sinners to be His "close family." Nothing can defile this "husband among His people," because the people *are* His bride! Jesus renders holy all that He chooses. Jesus confirms this principle in His willingness to touch the woman with an issue of blood (Lev. 15:25–27). By the way, this is one reason why Jesus cannot be married. He does not offer Himself as a husband to one physical wife, because He offers Himself as a Husband to His people, the church. We will discuss this more thoroughly in the next chapter.

Jesus allows nothing to keep Him from those He loves. When it comes to women, He does not let any social expectations keep Him from relating to them in love—not protocol, Jewish opinion, personal inconvenience, fatigue, suffering, or even contact with the dead. All His Christian sisters are like "virgin sisters who are near to Him because they have no husband."

It is so important for us as Christian women to realize the relationship that Christ claims in our lives. You may be a virgin, a widow, a prostitute, a mother, or a barren woman, but if you belong to Christ, you have a husband you can count on. His love sustains and guards you.

Two Exceptions

Our picture of Jesus as tender and gentle with women is shattered on two occasions. In two cases Jesus seems abrupt, almost rude. One is in His dealings with a Syrian woman who comes looking for Jesus to help her demon-possessed daughter.

The "Dog" (Matt. 15:21–28)

A non-Jewish, Syrian woman runs to Jesus when she hears He is in her town. Closing in on Him, she begins urgently crying for help. Jesus ignores the cries for such a long time that the disciples get weary of hearing her. When they beg Him to send her away, Jesus gives a curious reply. He says to the apostles in her hearing, "I was sent only to the lost sheep of the house of Israel" (Matt. 15:24). Undaunted, the woman falls at Jesus' feet and explains the dire predicament of her daughter. But Jesus remains unmoved. "It is not right to take the children's bread and throw it to the dogs," is His surprising reply.

Why is this tenderhearted Savior suddenly so cruel to this woman? Is He the Savior of the Jews only? Here at least, it would seem, we have an example of bigoted Christianity squashing a woman.

But Jesus does not break character. His response to this woman is not cruel, though it seems to be. On the contrary, Jesus sees in her such great faith that He knows she will hold firm as He tests it (John 6:64). Her faith will also provide a lesson to all present. In throwing up a roadblock to her faith, Jesus strengthens that faith while showing the Jews, who have rejected His message, how readily even the pagans believe.

The woman argues back with a powerful, humble, and clever response: "Even the dogs get crumbs." She sees that Jesus has so many riches to dispense that her daughter's case, though all-important to her, is only a "crumb" for Jesus. In His seemingly harsh response, Jesus honors this Syrian woman, holding up her faith as an example to all.

Mary: What Have I to Do with You?

The other woman to whom Jesus speaks in a seemingly heartless way is His own mother, Mary. The first occasion is when Mary and Joseph lose twelve-year-old Jesus, who has stayed behind after a festival day in Jerusalem to discuss the Scriptures with the rabbis in the temple. His parents travel for a full day before realizing that Jesus is not with the home-town crowd. (This has been a great comfort to me! Each of our seven children has been lost at least once.) After three more days of searching Jerusalem, they finally find Him in the temple. When Mary reprimands Jesus, the young man replies, "Don't you know I have to be about my Father's business?" (see Luke 2:49).

On a second occasion, Jesus, His disciples, and His family are invited to a wedding reception, where the wine runs out. Mary tells Jesus, who replies, "What has this concern of yours to do with Me, woman? . . . My hour has not yet come" (John 2:3–5).

On a third occasion, Jesus is preaching and healing when His mother and brothers come to find Him. When His family hears His teaching, they think He is out of his mind and come to rescue Him and get Him home (Mark 3:21). Matthew tells us of the exchange: "He was still speaking to the crowds when suddenly His mother and brothers were standing outside wanting to speak to Him. But He replied . . . 'Who is My mother, and who are My brothers?' And stretching out His hand toward His disciples, He said, 'Here are My mother and My brothers! For whoever does the will of My Father in heaven, that person is My brother and sister and mother'" (Matt. 12:46–50).

In a similar vein, Jesus contradicts a woman who wishes to honor Mary above other women. When a woman in the crowd calls out, "Blessed is the womb that bore you, and the breasts at which you nursed!" Jesus replies, "Blessed rather are those who hear the word of God and keep it!" (Luke 11:27–28 ESV). In all the Scripture accounts, Jesus never calls Mary His mother.

How can a perfect son treat His mother this way? The answer lies in the purpose of Jesus' ministry and death. His attitude to Mary is consistent from the youthful incident in the temple to His dying moment on the cross. Single-mindedly focused on the Father's schedule, He will not allow His physical mother to determine His plans, however well-intentioned her motivations.

Jesus is keenly aware of human tendencies to esteem people for the wrong reasons. Mary plays a minor role in the Gospel accounts because she must not become the focal point of Jesus' ministry or the object of glory, for the sake of the church and for her own sake. Mary *is* honored to bear, nurse, and raise Jesus. When Jesus is still *in utero*, the Holy Spirit stirs another unborn baby, John, to leap for joy and prompts Elizabeth to shout: "Blessed are you among women, and blessed is the fruit of your womb! . . . And blessed is she who believed that there would be a fulfillment of what was spoken to her from the Lord" (Luke 1:41–45 ESV).

In His abrupt expressions, Jesus is not denying that Mary is blessed, but He is teaching Mary not to rely on her physical relationship to Him. His eternal family is not necessarily His flesh-and-blood family. Those who do His will are His sisters, mothers, and brothers. By faith, each believer has a *more intimate* relationship with Christ through faith than Mary has with Him as His physical mother. Mary *herself* can only truly know her son by faith, not by the human links that tie her to Jesus.

Every mention of Jesus' relationship to Mary shows us that she cannot find a place in God's kingdom just because she is Jesus' birth mother. The physical birth proves that Jesus is truly a son of Adam and that the Son of God comes to live in sinful flesh because "He had to be like His brothers in every way" (Heb. 2:17). Jesus does not want anyone, *especially* Mary, to rely on the flesh for glory. If Mary is to brag of her physical role as mother, she can brag only in the fact that she has given Jesus a body of sinful flesh! For Jesus to encourage her in any way to rely on that fact as a reason for personal hope of salvation would be to deceive her most cruelly.

Jesus adamantly insists that Mary, whom He loves so dearly, must understand how to be unified to Him forever. If she wants to be in His family, she must, like all her sisters and brothers, enter that family by faith alone.

Jesus Establishes a Woman's Place in the Church

Jesus' seven dying words from the cross are rightly held up as programmatic, but how are we to understand Jesus' heartrending words to His mother: "Woman, behold, your son!" (John 19:26 ESV)? Is Jesus simply remembering at the last minute to provide for His mother's care after His death? Is he reminding John of some agreement to look after Mary if and when Jesus should die?

Mary stands at the foot of the cross, staring intently at her physical son, Jesus, whose death she mourns. But, again, Jesus turns her eyes away from the physical relationship she has with Him. He wants her to know that she is not losing a son. It is only His death that allows Mary to be His true mother, His spiritual mother. Without the death and resurrection of her son, Mary would have no hope of eternal life or of entering the kingdom of God. In fact, she would have no hope of being with Him forever.

Jesus deliberately directs Mary's eyes away from His own dying form to focus them on John, at her side. Jesus is saying to Mary that His death provides her a true family—John and the other disciples, all of whom are His mothers, sisters, and brothers. If she wants to be a true mother to Jesus, she will be a mother to John. Ultimately, she will not lose either Jesus or John, since Jesus' resurrection proves His power over death.

Here is the only time Jesus uses the word *mother* in speaking of Mary, and He uses it to tell John, "Behold, *your* mother" (John 19:27 ESV, emphasis added). Mary, and all women with her, now step into a new role. No longer can any woman hope to be the mother of the Savior by physically bearing Him and bringing Him into the world. Just as John the Baptist was the last of the prophets, so Mary is the last of the Old Testament mothers, for when she is chosen to bear Jesus, the promise to Eve is fulfilled. On the cross and at the resurrection, the seed of Eve crushes the head of the serpent. But Mary is also the first of the New Testament mothers.

Jesus' first miracle is at a wedding, where He makes seven hundred liters of wine in celebration of the establishment of a family (John 2:1–11). One of His last words from the cross establishes a new family, in which He is the husband and believers are the wife. At the cross, Mary is present at the betrothal of her son, who pays with His life to purchase His bride. On that day, Jesus does not yet drink from the cup of celebration wine. The wine that flows that day is plentiful, but it is the bitter cup of God's judgment that Jesus drinks for us all.

It is the wine of His blood, poured out for us. One day, the celebratory wine of Jesus' wedding feast will also flow in joy, when the marriage is consummated and Jesus comes back to collect His bride and take her home forever. We don't look for a physical seed from Jesus, by Mary Magdalene or anyone else.

Jesus' bride is the church—all those who relate to Him by faith. As we examine the bride of Christ, the church, we will see why the marriage structure is not destroyed, but is set into a different context.

Jesus' words to Mary from the cross show us her role and the role that women after her will take on. Jesus does not set her up as the mother of the church par excellence. He does not ask her to be an apostle, to be John's teacher, or to answer the prayers of the church on His behalf. He simply asks her to be a mother to John and, by implication, to other disciples. After Jesus dies, rises, and ascends to heaven, Mary, like all Christian women, exercises her "mothering" of Christ by mothering others in Christ's church.

It is also important that Jesus asks John to be her son. Mary is not only giving, but receiving. She is a normal, ordinary, sinful woman who is purchased by the blood of Jesus and placed in Christ's family line by faith. Jesus' women ancestors were sinners. His physical mother is a sinner, and His spiritual descendants are sinners. All believers, whether women or men, are the "bride" of Christ, made holy by Him to bear descendants "set apart" and made holy to God. Christ and the church are the new Adam and Eve, the founding couple for a new humanity. Their union produces offspring for God by the power of the Holy Spirit.

The success of a novel like the *Da Vinci Code* shows how many people are intrigued with the possibility that Jesus had a sexual relationship with Mary Magdalene, but Jesus would never have compromised His commitment to His chosen bride, the church. Christ's descendants are adopted into God's family by faith. The Old Testament picture of a physical seed becomes a broader river of blessing in Christ. Anyone, from any nation and any birth line can be brought into the family of God by faith in Jesus Christ's death and resurrection.

Here we see the beginning of the new role for women. Until now, women have been longing to bear the Messiah. Now that the promise has been fulfilled, they are to be mothers and sisters in the body of Christ, the church. How does this new "spiritual mothering" role fit into God's plan for a new humanity, now that the promise to Eve has been fulfilled? Is a woman's physical seed still important? Is her identity *as a woman* still tied to marriage, or does it become completely spiritual? In the next chapters, we will see how Jesus' death and resurrection both maintain and expand the woman's creation calling.

■ ■ ■

Discussion Questions

1. What are the dangers of giving Mary too much honor? Too little honor?

2. Does it change your attitude to know that Jesus receives your "mothering" and "sistering" whenever you encourage other women?

3. Christian men will never love women the way Jesus did. Is it a woman's job to point this out? Why or why not?

4. How can you be a witness to Jesus' death and resurrection in your life as a woman?

5. How do you find intellectual refreshment in your faith?

6. How does Jesus show His love to you between His ascension and His return?

7. How can you provide financial and practical help to Jesus?

8. Jesus broke social stigmas to meet women's needs. Should we break social stigmas today? If so, which ones? Why?

9. Have you needed to be "rude" for the sake of the gospel? Should we use the kind of language Jesus did with the Syro-Phoenician woman? Why or why not?

10. How can you be true to your calling as a woman in the new family Christ created—the church?

■　■　■

Resources

Beeke, Joel. *Bringing the Gospel to Covenant Children.* Reformation Heritage Books, n.d.

Burns, Jabez. *Mothers of the Wise and Good.* Vestavia Hills, Ala.: Solid Ground Christian Books, 2001.

Elliot, Elisabeth. *Let Me Be a Woman.* Carol Stream, Ill.: Tyndale, 1999.

Grudem, Wayne, ed. *Biblical Foundations for Manhood and Womanhood.* Wheaton, Ill.: Crossway, 2002.

Hunt, Susan. *Spiritual Mothering: The Titus 2 Model for Women Mentoring Women.* Wheaton, Ill.: Crossway, 1992.

Knight, George W. *The Role Relationship of Men and Women: New Testament Teaching.* Chicago: Moody Press, 1985.

*Earthly marriage as it is now lived out
is a bad copy of a good original.*

—GEOFFREY W. BROMILEY

9

■■■■■

The Bride

THE FAMOUS BASEBALL PLAYER, Ted Williams, left a dying wish to have his body frozen in liquid nitrogen, using a process know as cryonics. "Cryonicists donate their bodies for freezing—or sometimes just their heads—in the belief that scientific breakthroughs still hundreds of years away will allow doctors to regenerate youthful bodies from DNA."[1]

Buried in the heart of every human being is the dream of living forever, but only one human being has exerted power over death, emerging from His own tomb. His body passed through the burial shroud and walked out of the grave. This body was unique, physical yet also spiritual. In the body of the resurrected Jesus, the elements of creation were reconstituted in a miraculous way unknown to cryonics experts. Jesus promises to transform the bodies of all those who are His brothers and sisters in faith.

At the resurrection of Jesus, the Holy Spirit, whose breath created the first man, breathes life into the first new man. When Jesus ascends to heaven, He sends that same Spirit to create a new humanity, who will receive the same kind of body as the one in which Jesus walked away from the grave.

In this new world order, some of the pre-Jesus structures fall away. God's presence is no longer defined by the ark of the covenant, the holy city of Jerusalem, the sacrificial system, or the priestly order. Through the Spirit, the presence of God lives in all believers, who become prophets, priests, and kings. God the Spirit is on the march with the good news that Christ has come to save sinners. In the postresurrection people of God, women take part in a new way in the expansion of Christ's kingdom. The gospel transcends all social categories—slave or master, Jew or Greek, woman or man.

Jesus Pours Out His Spirit on Women

Women were already an integral part of Jesus' ministry team before His death, and their fidelity did not end at the cross. They followed Jesus' arrest and crucifixion closely. Though the disciples do not at first believe them, the women are the first eyewitnesses of the resurrected Jesus. In the first crucial hours of the church's birth, the community of believers is tight knit and is further unified by the tumultuous and frightening events of crucifixion week. The faithful women are probably present when Jesus appears to His disciples as a group. They may follow the male disciples to the scene of the ascension, not far from Mary and Martha's home in Bethany. When Peter says, "God has resurrected this Jesus. We are all witnesses of this" (Acts 2:32), he surely includes those female believers who were the very first to see the risen LORD and upon whom the Holy Spirit came at Pentecost (Acts 1:1–14; Matt. 28:1–6).

Jesus' mother, Mary, is specifically mentioned. This shows us that she understood Jesus' dying words to her and had adopted the church family as her own. In the early chapters of Acts, we read that the fledgling band of believers is together when the Holy Spirit falls on them.

Tongues of fire appear on the heads of both men and women. The sound of a roaring wind draws crowds from the neighborhood; something supernatural is happening. Those who gather hear both male and female disciples speaking in foreign languages about the power of God, who raised Jesus from the dead.

We cannot argue that the Spirit comes only on the apostles, since Peter explains what is happening by quoting the prophet Joel: "Your sons and your daughters will prophesy . . . I will even pour out My Spirit on My male and female slaves in those days, and they will prophesy" (Acts 2:17–18; Joel 2:28–32). Women, with men, are gifted by the Spirit to speak in foreign languages "the magnificent acts of God."

So much changes. Yet much does not. We don't have our resurrection bodies yet, and Jesus instructs us, through His apostles, about living in our old bodies. Jesus leaves three major structures in place: governments, the church, and the family. He advocates paying taxes and refuses to allow His disciples to lead a political movement against the Roman oppressors. "Give to Caesar what is Caesar's and to God what is God's," He says. Victory does not mean an immediate theocracy. He establishes the authority of the church, giving His apostles a commission to preach, teach, and baptize in His name. He gives them the authority of His own name to control spiritual powers and to accomplish kingdom purposes.

In establishing His church, Jesus makes specific appearances to the male apostles (Acts 1:2–3) and reserves words of commissioning for them. Jesus "breathed on them and said, 'Receive the Holy Spirit. If you forgive anyone his sins, they are forgiven; if you do not forgive them, they are not forgiven'" (John 20:22–23 NIV). At the ascension, the angels speak specifically to the men: "Men of Galilee, why do you stand looking into heaven?" (Acts 1:11 ESV).

The third authority structure that Jesus leaves in place when He ascends to heaven is marriage and the family. Jesus often instructs converts to return home to tell what He has done for them. He returns a little girl to the care of her parents, and a son to the care of his mother. He reprimands the Pharisees for neglecting their elderly parents (Mark 7:11–13). After making the point that He answers only to His heavenly Father, the twelve-year-old Jesus upholds the family by submitting to the authority of Mary and Joseph. The sinless one, God made man, submits to parents who are weak sinners (Luke 2:51). Jesus celebrates a wedding and does not challenge the marriage structure. Jesus never says about marriage, "You have heard it said that a man will leave his father and mother and be united to his wife, but I say to you that a man and woman are no longer to be united in marriage." Jesus affirms marriage, breathing into it new meaning and power. God established marriage at creation, and it is not to be destroyed by men.

In the New Covenant, men and women serve Jesus in love as His own sisters, mothers, and brothers by infusing their daily lives with the joy that comes from His forgiveness and the power that comes from His Spirit. Jesus asks His followers to be *willing* to leave husbands, wives, fathers, mothers, or children for His sake, but generally, He expects believers to serve Him in the context of their families.

The Already and the Not Yet

In considering the role of a woman in the church and family, we must respect both what *has* changed and what has *not* changed. Women are a natural part of the community and its witness, yet Jesus affirms the authority of men in their families and in the church. The community of believers, as a unit, receives Jesus' teaching both before and after his resurrection. Women are integrally involved in ministry, equally valued by Christ for their service, and are filled with the Holy Spirit. However, Jesus appoints men to guard the deposit of the gospel. Jesus wants women to stay married and to fulfill the role He designed from the beginning.

Jesus tells His disciples that His ascension is necessary so that the Holy Spirit can come to live in the church, which honors Christ and shows His glory to a watching world. After the resurrection, women live their created roles as wives and mothers in the light of the Christian gospel. As they are made new in Christ, they have a far greater understanding and power than the women in the Old Testament. They begin to understand and live their lives as women in the way God intended from the beginning.

Male-female relationships are not destroyed when Jesus comes. God is not finished with the marriage structure yet because *He uses marriage to show us about the church's relationship to Him.* As we look at our own marriages, we understand a little about Christ's love for the church but, as Geoffrey Bromiley put it, "Earthly marriage as it is now lived out is a bad copy of a good original." As we analyze Christ's love for His bride, the church, we understand what our own marriages *should* be.

The Bride Finds Love Without Fear

From the beginning of human existence, there is marriage. The first woman is greeted by Adam's awe. Their marriage shows Adam and Eve that they are different from God, different from the animals, and different from each other. It also illustrates the deeper, broader, better, wider, greater love of God for them. God makes even the original marriage of Adam and Eve to show us the relationship between Jesus and His bride.

Until the Fall, Adam and Eve know true communion with each other because they know true communion with their Creator. A perfect man shows perfect love to a perfect wife. Adam and Eve begin the human journey in a *de facto* marriage, as male and female partners in blessing, to fulfill God's job description for them: be fruitful and multiply, fill the earth, subdue and rule over it. They are in an indissoluble relationship, made by God. Thus blessed, they are a blessing to each other, to the animals and to the earth, with which they have a relation-ship as good caretakers.

This first human relationship is the structural model God lays down for human beings. As mankind falls into sin and marriage becomes more a prison than a paradise, marriage is not abandoned by God. Marriage, even in its corrupted state, still represents the *summum* of human love and fellowship and is a general blessing to mankind, as is the sun that warms us or the rain that produces a harvest. God preserves marriage for our good, but also because He does not want this powerful image of His love to disappear. All through God's revelation, God uses marriage imagery to show us about His love to His people. We must understand this deeper marriage structure if we hope to understand God's design for women.

The Grand Pursuit: Christ Seeks His Bride

The theme of God's marriage to His people runs from Genesis to Revelation. The Bible uses sexual and wedding imagery constantly. The young Jewish virgin represents spiritual purity. Thus priests are to marry only virgins. Once married, neither a wife nor a husband is to run after other partners or other gods. The wife's fidelity is a pic-ture of the spiritual fidelity God's people owe Him. Their infidelity is described as "harlotry." God created us to understand the notion of sexual purity. Thus, feminine purity and profligacy are good images of spiritual fidelity or apostasy.

A husband's faithful love is a picture of God's fidelity to His people. The bride cannot escape her husband, who pursues her down the halls of history. Guilty, she hides from Him in the Garden of Eden. She is pursued through the wanderings of Abraham in pagan territory and during her long imprisonment in Pharaoh's land. Her lack of faithful-ness in the desert wanderings cannot shake her suitor's love, nor can her dreary idolatry during the times of the judges, when she worships the sun, moon, and stars instead of her heavenly lover. She cannot escape His love through the years of unfaithful kings and corrupt prophets; through the time of estrangement when she weeps in the captivity of foreign powers. She cannot hide from Him anywhere.

Finally, He descends to earth and condescends to be born of a woman, a virgin. Jesus Christ, the glorious son of the King, has left His rich halls to wander homeless through His kingdom, unrecognized, unclothed, dishonored, and despised—all for the sake of His bride. Since she has sold herself into slavery under the wicked one, He dies to buy her back, and rises in power to take her to His own kingdom.

This is the drama of a good romance. Where do we get our ideals of unrequited love, of sacrificial, all-or-nothing passion? All we know of true love comes ultimately from the love that Jesus Christ manifests in His princely search for His bride. However, Jesus' quest differs from the Prince Charming model. He doesn't seek a beautiful bride whose poverty only disguises her true royalty. He chooses a harlot, sets His love on her, and bestows on her all the beauty she needs.

In the first chapter of this book, we saw the discouraging reality of human relationships. There are no men whom women can trust, and there are no women whom men can trust. Absolute fidelity exists nowhere in this broken world. However, there is one man totally committed to His bride and in whom she will never be disappointed. In this husband she finds all her heart's desires. What does the bride find when she looks to her heavenly lover?

The Bride Finds Protection from Danger

In the movie, the *Return of the King,* the hobbit Sam accidentally slides down a rocky slope just as enemy soldiers are marching by. Hearing the noise, they approach Sam, who is in plain view. Sam's master, Frodo, scrambles down after him and throws his Elvin cloak over both of them. Its magical qualities make the hump of hobbits look exactly like a boulder, and the enemy soldiers move away, puzzled, unable to see what is right under their noses.

The church hides under Jesus' cloak of protection, under which she is safe from all harm. Tucked under God's wing, covered by His shield, the church is safe. Under Christ's protective cloak we are hidden from the "dark lord" of this earth, hidden from the evil eye that seeks to destroy us. We are protected from temptation and harm to our souls. The fiery darts of the wicked one cannot reach us.

A wife can place such faith, on a human level, in her husband. She trusts him to protect her physically, to protect her financially, to watch out for her good. As long as his strength remains, he will hide her under his cloak of protection. The physical and material protection a husband offers his wife is the least important element of his calling; but it is certainly the most elementary, instinctive, and obvious.

How our country allows eighteen-year-old girls to "man" machine guns in defense of our national interests, while able-bodied men sit home watching football games is beyond my comprehension. In their desire to prove themselves worthy of equal treatment by the guys, these women sometimes abandon all sense of modesty and morality. What a shock to our American soul it was to see a young *woman* delighting in the sexual harassment of Iraqi prisoners. Why does it take such a shocking incident to make us realize that women do not belong on the front lines?

In addition, sending women to war tends to denigrate the courage of our young men, discouraging them from stepping into the role of defenders. If we continue, our society may one day look like the Israel in which Old Testament Deborah lived. Bemoaning the military cowardice of men, she asked, "Was shield or spear to be seen among forty thousand in Israel?" (Judg. 5:8 ESV).

Why do we women fall for the lie that it is shameful to accept the physical provision and protection of a caring husband? Women *are* physically weaker than men. Why reject their help? Of course, in an emergency, a woman can step up to do "a man's job," but in allowing a husband to protect and care for her, a woman is following a model set up by God. The apostle Paul says that a man who looks after his wife is looking after his own body, in the most instinctive, natural, and created way. In fact, if he does not treat a woman as the "weaker vessel," his very prayers will be hindered (1 Pet. 3:7). A woman who refuses the tender help of her husband is hindering her husband's prayers.

The Bride Takes Shelter from Judgment

God's people hide under His covering not only for physical protection, but for protection from judgment. God's holy nature is more than the bride can bear. She needs protection from His burning purity. God hides Moses in the "cleft of a rock" while His glory passes by. Moses is covered by the hand of God (Exod. 33:22). God warns Aaron "not to come whenever he chooses into the Most Holy Place behind the curtain in front of the atonement cover on the ark, or else he will die, because I appear in the cloud over the atonement cover" (Lev. 16:2 NIV).

When the Israelites wander through the desert with the ark of the covenant, symbolizing God's presence with them, the ark is to be protected and kept holy. Those who protected it were "Moses and Aaron and his sons, guarding the sanctuary itself, to protect the people of Israel" (Num. 3:38 ESV). For all its oddities, the movie *Raiders of the Lost Ark* has the right idea. The ark, because it represented God's holiness, can and sometimes does break out against people (Uzzah, and the Philistines, for example).

God tells the people to make a covering for the ark—two cherubim, whose wings hover over it. Symbolically, they protect the people, keeping God's holiness from breaking out to destroy them, because holiness cannot bear unholiness. When the high priest comes to offer the sacrifice each year, he adds another layer of protection, filling the area with smoke, so that even the cherubim are covered. The instructions to

Aaron are to "put the incense on the fire before the LORD, that the cloud of the incense may cover the mercy seat that is over the testimony, so that he does not die" (Lev. 16:13 ESV). So dangerous is God's holiness that the high priest himself must not see even the angels who are covering the box that represents God's presence!

This is not ritual hocus pocus. There is a stunning, awesome, fearful reality to God's holiness. The holy is a raging fire that devours the unholy: "The sinners in Zion are terrified; trembling grips the godless: 'Who of us can dwell with the consuming fire? Who of us can dwell with everlasting burning?'" (Isa. 33:14 NIV).

One day, God's holy fury does break out against His people in full force. On that day, the cherubim, the smoke, and the curtain can no longer protect the sinner. God's judgment bursts forth, tearing the curtain that hangs in front of the holy of holies, where the ark is kept, and spreading a cloud right over the sun to blacken it (Matt. 27:51–53). The holy anger of God does not destroy His people, however. It falls on a substitute, the holy man, Jesus. In taking the full force of God's judgment, Jesus provides protection for His church. It is His robe of righteousness that fulfills the psalmist's prayer: "Spread your protection over them, that those who love your name may exult in you. For . . . you cover [the righteous] with favor as with a shield" (Ps. 5:11–12 ESV).

The faithless bride no longer fears judgment from a holy husband because He has paid the bride price for her and covered her with a protective robe. When God looks at the church, covered by Christ's robe, He no longer sees an enemy, but a beautifully perfect and righteous bride. She can enter His presence without fear of destruction, because she is made holy.

In the scriptural approach to marriage, a wife hides under the protection of her husband as the church hides under the robe of Christ. Of course, it is not the husband's righteousness that redeems his wife from her sins, nor does he ultimately answer for her to the Judge on that final judgment day. She will answer God for her own sin, just as Eve had to answer individually for her part in the Fall. However, the Scripture implies that husbands are partially responsible for the holiness of their wives, insofar as they are given the task of watching over and protecting their wives' spiritual nurturing.

A wife respects a husband who is willing to protect her from ungodliness as well as physical harm. She will see such a husband pleading for her before God's throne of grace, pouring out prayers for her holiness. She will see him working tirelessly to encourage her faithfulness to God and her service to His kingdom. She will not be able to deter him from righteousness by feminine wiles, greed, jealousy, or gossip. He will ferociously protect their relationship and not allow lust or complacency to tear it down. In love, he will resist her when she falls prey to sinful tendencies, and will clothe her so that her Christlike royalty will shine out.

Here is how God, the gracious and protective husband deals with His bride:

"I spread the corner of my garment over you and covered
your nakedness; I made my vow to you and entered into a
covenant with you, declares the Lord GOD, and you became
mine. Then I bathed you with water and washed off your
blood from you and anointed you with oil. I clothed you
also with embroidered cloth and shod you with fine leather.
I wrapped you in fine linen and covered you with silk. And I
adorned you with ornaments and put bracelets on your wrists
and a chain on your neck. And I put a ring on your nose and
earrings in your ears and a beautiful crown on your head.
Thus you were adorned with gold and silver, and your clothing was of fine linen and silk and embroidered cloth. You ate
fine flour and honey and oil. You grew exceedingly beautiful
and advanced to royalty" (Ezek. 16:8–13 ESV).

Paul picks up parallels to this passage when he instructs husbands to care for their wives as for their own bodies. The woman is kept safe and holy under that covering, but only because the marriage structure shows us the deeper structure of the church's protection under the robe of Christ. The husband's covering is a symbol of the covering protection and sanctifying presence of God Himself.

Marriage carries such a high representative quality that God is incensed when men use the power of their ability to "cover" a woman with violence or hard-heartedness. His anger is fierce: "The man who hates and divorces . . . covers his garment with violence. . . . So guard yourselves in your spirit, and do not be faithless" (Mal. 2:16 ESV).

The Christian man who abuses his authority to cause suffering to his wife, sometimes even physical pain, gives evidence of a sickening corruption of God's design and will be most harshly punished by God, since such cruelty is a slander to the name of God. If a Christian husband ever falls prey to such behavior, the church must react urgently to protect the woman and thus defend God's holy reputation.

The Bride Bathes in Love

The church bathes in the love of Jesus that washes her clean. The apostle Paul argues that Christ, the head of the church and its Savior, washes His bride. The church needs cleansing just as the young girl in Ezekiel 16 needed to be washed and clothed. Jesus purifies His bride by giving His life for her and in this sense He makes her morally pure, a perfect bride. Just as the church can look to Christ for purification, so, on a human level, a wife looks to her husband to be washed clean by the Word:

Husbands, love your wives, just as also Christ loved the church and gave Himself for her, to make her holy, cleansing her in the washing of water by the word. He did this to present the church to Himself in splendor, without spot or wrinkle or any such thing, but holy and blameless. In the same way, husbands should love their wives as their own bodies. He who loves his wife loves himself. For no one ever hates his own flesh, but provides and cares for it, just as Christ does for the church, since we are members of His body (Eph. 5:25–30).

A wife whose husband understands this principle can trust him to work for her purity. She can humbly listen to him and accept his advice, rather than seeking her own stubborn way. The godly husband represents Christ as he takes on the human task of "washing" his wife in the Word.

The bride is holy in another way. She is not only purified; she is also "set apart" for Christ. She belongs to Him, as His unique treasure. He makes her holy by choosing her, just as certain utensils in the Old Testament were holy because they were made and set apart for use in the temple. God commands the prophet Hosea to pursue a prostitute as his wife, setting her apart for holiness. In the passage cited from Ezekiel, a young man rescues an abandoned baby girl from the side of the road. He provides for her, clothes her, and gives her all she needs until she matures, when he returns to marry her. He has set his love on this girl. She is "set apart" for him.

A woman should not fear having a husband who has set his love on her. He participates in God's plan to make her holy by determining to love her and her alone. There is no shame in receiving such love! God sets His love on His bride, creating a cosmic family, of which our human families are a picture. She is "set apart" to Him alone—holy, sanctified, precious. The children of that holy marriage are also set apart for God and made holy in this sense.

The Bride Is Refreshed by Christ's Love

In addition to protection from danger and judgment; in addition to the cleansing water of the Word of God, Christ's bride finds strength and new life in His love. The church breathes in the life and power of

Christ's resurrection, without which she would be as dry and dead as the bones scattered across the valley in Ezekiel's vision. Jesus' prophetic word raises dead sinners, puts sinews and flesh back on their bones, and gives them an immortal body and a perfected soul. The husband is truly the Creator, both of original earthly life and of the new men and women of the world to come.

A woman does not look to her human husband for regeneration, but she does find refreshment, comfort, and renewed strength in his strength and love. It is a happy woman who lives in a home where her husband bathes himself in God's Word and creates a Word-soaked atmosphere for fun and work. In that home, she derives spiritual power, joy, and hope— through her husband and from the Lord. Just as the church drinks up the love and truth that Jesus offers—that living water that cheers and energizes the soul—so a wife's soul is revived by a husband whose love she trusts. As husband and wife grow old together, their bodies waste away, but their souls are renewed by each other, day by day.

In this atmosphere, a wife will, in turn, create hope and joy in her husband. As she, too, clings to the power of God's Word and draws strength from the resurrection power of the Holy Spirit living in her, she lifts the discouraged head of her husband and inspires him to carry on, trusting in God's care and love for His people. The prophetic voice of women who bathe in the Scriptures is ever present in the Bible, beginning with the triumphant shout of Eve, "Behold, I have born a man, Jehovah!" (see Gen. 4:1), and ending in the final call of the bride of Christ in Revelation, calling to all to come and drink of the water of life (Rev. 22:17). However, Paul teaches that the primary responsibility as administrator of the Word falls on the husband.

The Bride Trusts Christ's Enduring Love

The church can rely on the solidity of Christ's love. It never quits. It will last forever because Jesus is the beginning and the end of all things, the same yesterday, today, and forever. This absolute faithfulness and dependability is the hope of Christ's bride. Everyone knows that Christians still have plenty of wrinkles. Though the death of Christ has already put the true church (children of God by faith in the work of Christ)[2] in a position of legal innocence, the wrinkles are still being smoothed out.

My grandson Liam was two when he examined my face carefully and said, "Grandma, you have angry eyebrows." His four-year-old brother, Jesse, piped up, "*and* an Eeyore mouth!" My Eeyore mouth and my angry eyebrows are set in a face with plenty of wrinkles, for which I bought an expensive skin cream which is supposed to make them look fewer and shallower each day. The problem is, it doesn't work. But Christ's love really does remove wrinkles! Not the physical ones, but the moral ones that make us recoil in horror when we look in the mirror of God's Word. Only the rejuvenating power of Christ's anointing oil of faithful eternal love will present the church as a gorgeous, wrinkle-free bride for the King when He throws His extravagant cosmic wedding party in the new creation world.

Women who benefit from the love of a Christian husband see a weak human reflection of that faithful love. A Christian husband will not give up on his wife, no matter how difficult and obnoxious she is, no matter how overweight she has become, no matter how many wrinkles appear on her once-lovely face. The Christian husband, knowing that he has been loved and rescued and made holy, is given the eyes of Christ, who sees in the church no inherent beauty, but a beauty that has been bestowed on her as a gift. By God's power, the Christian husband bestows on his wife the gift of beauty, exercising fidelity for the sake of Christ, and rejecting temptations to look at more beautiful women or to long for a life that God has not chosen for him.

We know a man who set his love on a young woman and married her. She left him for another man. This Christian gentleman decided that he had the freedom in Christ to take his ex-wife back. She left him again, and again our friend took her back. Many shook their heads in disapproval, but this decision, born of fidelity, is a picture of what God our husband has done for us. This miraculous and undeserved love, fed by the streams of God's grace, is what Christianity offers to the debate on women and marriage. Our hope plunges its roots not into male fidelity, but into the depth of God's promises.

The Bride Keeps Her Identity in Christ

The parallels between the church-Christ relationship and the wife-husband relationship teach us about a woman's identity. God's Word encourages us to connect the dots when it sets out an image for us to explore. Eve is drawn from Adam's side, and the church is drawn from Christ's side. Eve receives her name from Adam, just as the church receives Christ's name. The church is rescued by Christ's sacrifice of Himself for her, just as Adam . . . but no. Adam failed to sacrifice himself for Eve. Instead, he plunged into sin with her. A Christian husband, by the wisdom and power of Christ, will see how to lay down his life for his wife.

In the church-Christ relationship, unity does not destroy the identity of the church or of Christ. The union of love between Christ and His bride respects and maintains the differences between them. Here is no experience of "becoming one with the universe." The church is made of created human beings who remain creatures even in heaven. This separateness is a holy reality that Christianity brings to the subject of male-female relationships. The union and communion of a man and his wife does not deny, but rather emphasizes, their sexual differences. A man remains a man. A woman remains a woman. It is those very differences that allow such close communion. Without difference, we cannot have communion, for we blend into an indistinguishable nothingness.

Christ does not destroy but establishes the identity of the church. A husband does not destroy the identity of his wife, but rather establishes it. In her respect for him, as she receives his name, as she allows him to shape her godliness by his careful instruction and love, she finds herself more of a woman, with a greater sense of value. Her individual gifts are valued. She is treasured and honored.

We women have listened too long to the poisonous whispers of our culture. It is not demeaning to "belong" to a husband. It is no humiliation to take on his name. It is not an assault on our identity to be "defined" as a man's wife. He was born of a woman and recognizes the honor and value of women in his life, whether blood sisters and mother, or spiritual sisters and mothers. Christian women need to start speaking up about the honor and privilege we have to accept the protection, the bath of holiness, the definition of an honorable name that our marriages give us. These gracious gifts are from God as a very imperfect picture of the identity, love, honor, and protection that Christ bestows on His bride.

The Bride Seeks Close Communion with Christ

It is the church's goal to be in communion with her Savior and Lord. She is not to cut herself off and attempt to lead an independent life in her own strength. This is the pride and arrogance that plunged Eve and the whole human race with her into dark despair. Eve decided that God's idea about the structure of the world was somehow lacking and that she could improve upon it. Her attempt to bring humanity to a higher level plunged all humans after her into misery, depression, guilt, war, violence, and loneliness. Independence does not bring fulfillment, but destruction.

In Jesus, God comes down with a road map to peace. To accomplish the peace, He has the power to change hearts, to conquer hate, and to produce love, life, and joy. The whole purpose of the church is to delight in God and to live in happy communion with Him. As Christians are united to Him, they will accomplish God's peace plan in their own lives and on the planet and will discover the exhilaration of fulfillment and the establishment of their identity.

In this aspect as well, a marriage reflects the deeper truth of the relationship between Christ and His church. It is a wife's joy and goal to be in communion with her husband. She is to understand his desires and work toward accomplishing them. She is to begin conforming her thoughts to his, knowing his likes and dislikes, taking on his "image" in a certain sense. She does not worship or idolize him. That he is a sinner, she will have no trouble seeing. But as she submits to him in everything (Eph. 5:24), as Paul puts it, she relies on the strength of the Lord to infuse her heart with compassion, power, courage, hope, joy, and fidelity, in order to please God by pleasing her husband. As she seeks communion with him, she respects his ways and does not pre-define that communion.

Christian women are often guilty of defining godliness in their own feminine terms. To them, godliness means sitting by the fire and talking about "the relationship" for hours. It means crying or making small talk, or showing sensitivity. Though some men may need to learn to talk a little more, their godliness will not work itself out in the same ways as that of women. Masculine godliness will not appear as we women expect it to. Women must work hard to understand how God made men to function, rather than defining them according to our terms. If we expect men to take the time to understand us, we must be willing to understand how they see and live communion.

One way (not the only way) a married woman discovers deeper communion with God is discovering deeper communion with her husband. Sin builds barriers between males and females. In Christ, we have the power to destroy those walls of separation and to become one with our husbands without losing our identities.

The Bride Looks to Christ for Her Definition

The church does not boss Christ around. It is not up to the church to tell Christ how to run the universe, treat the ungodly, or order His plans for believers. The church submits to Christ's plans and conforms her heart to His direction. Christ has earned the right to direct the church in two ways: He created all things, and He bought the church at the cost of His life. She thus doubly belongs to Him. Because He made her, then rescued her from her tyrant owner and brought her home to be His bride, He dictates the terms.

If we fail to see Christ's absolute authority in our lives, we fail to understand the gospel. Purchased sinners have no rights, lay no claims, dictate no terms. In this sense, Christianity squashes not only women, but everyone! All humans are slaves to one master or another—either to worldly concerns or to Christ; either to the devil or to God. The apostle Paul paints the picture of Christ leading a triumphant army into the city. Paul is at the end of the line, like a slave whom conquering Roman generals would parade through the streets as proof of their victory over the enemy. These slaves were paraded into the arena, where they were put to death before the crowds. This is Paul's picture of our commitment to Christ. We have not "decided to let Jesus into our hearts."[3] We have been conquered by His love and are His captives, chained to the chariot of the victor, Christ.

Service to Jesus is not the same as service to the devil. Service to Christ is freedom, while service to the devil is an eternity of fear and horror. In calling our service slavery, Paul is emphasizing the radicality of the bonds. There is no escaping our service to Christ, but it is a service of love that leads to life. An Old Testament slave who loved his master would have his ear pierced, marking his desire to belong to the household for good. Such lifelong service to King Jesus is what Paul speaks of when he says, "For to me to live is Christ" (Phil. 1:21 KJV).

As the church is bound to Christ for eternity, so a wife is bound to her husband until those ties are dissolved for something better in heaven. While they are both alive, they are united by God and nothing is to separate them. Our culture's emphasis on rights and privileges has led to easy divorce, which apparently existed in Jesus' time as well, if the disciples' shock at Jesus' rigorous demands for marriage are any indication (Matt. 5:31–32).

In Christian marriage, a wife is wooed, won, and wed by the pro-active love of her husband, whom God has established as leader of the home. The husband's love drives the couple and the family. He is a vice-roy in the home, responsible for holding the unity of the home together and displaying God's rich love to his wife and children. I am fully aware of how radical such thinking sounds, but it is scriptural. God's Word is most clear! If we choose to countermand God's structures, we will pay the consequences in our own individual lives and as a society.

Christian Marriage and Sexual Chaos

At the dawn of the twenty-first century, marriage is up for grabs. Homosexual marriage is sanctioned in Massachusetts, and the battle to define marriage rages. Who gets to define it and why? The courts? National constitutions? Leagues of nations? The United Nations? Religious institutions? The will of the people? Why bother to define it? Perhaps marriage is the outdated convenience of tired cultures with less control over their reproduction and environment than we now have.

There is virtually no legal reason why marriage could not soon be recognized as any combination of individuals (without respect to gender or age) willing to enter a contractual agreement for a given period of time—a kind of social business partnership. Eventually, we could marry a snake, since we are all "earthkind" and the human race must learn morals from the deep principles of the earth itself. Pets now have passports in the European Union, and "pet carers" are willing to pay thousands of dollars to operate on them, clone them, cremate them, or designate them as heirs. Genetic manipulation may one day combine the animal with the human in a final countermanding of God's created order—a mixing of the species that may unite what God has put asunder.

Should we lay our reputations on the line for a one woman/one man-for-life marriage structure? Traditional marriage, we argue, offers stability to society, reduces the spread of venereal diseases and AIDS, gives children a greater chance of success in school and a lower statistical likelihood of criminal behavior. Such arguments may throw up a temporary protective shield for "traditional" marriage. However, they will not hold up for long against today's hybrid unions.

If we secure arguments for "old-fashioned" marriage by appealing to social effects alone, we will have no answer to the argument I recently heard on a Public Broadcasting program. On it, a researcher reasoned that the most creative and energetic communities were those whose population had the highest percentage of gays and lesbians. How will we defend traditional marriage if it is proven one day that the children of lesbians have a higher acceptance rate at Harvard, or that polygamous Mormons run more successful businesses than their one-wife-only colleagues?

Society *is* better off if it respects God's idea for marriage, but ultimately, we cannot defend marriage from the bottom up. We must argue not from pragmatism but from principle. We defend marriage because God made it for us and told us it is good. We defend it because God created it as a living picture of His own love for us. The human marriage contract depends on its heavenly model for solidity and meaning. If we strip marriage of its power by destroying the reality on which it is modeled, it will collapse lifeless, like Peter Pan's shadow, to be tucked away in a drawer of history. When marriage is cut off from its Christian meaning, we find few arguments to defend it. The very power of the structure can be twisted to evil ends. The source of love that makes marriage a blessing is the love of God for His people. True marriage is more than the bottle in which the wine is stored. It is the wine that fills the bottle.

Christians show Christ to the world *in their marriages.* If we are faithful to God's structures and live out our family lives before a watching world, we will not only affect the society by slowing down its precipitous moral slide, but will also illustrate the truth that has shone on us in Christ, the light of the world. That truth does not come from within, from our own instincts, from our feminine souls, from looking into the depths of our own being, or from looking to the soul of the universe. That truth is revealed to us from the outside, in the Scriptures and in the person of Jesus, who shattered time and history to be born of a woman in a stable (Luke 2:7).

As women, we bear witness to the glory of Christ by taking marriage as seriously as He does. We show the reality of Christ's love for His bride the church by respecting the human structures that are a picture of that love. If we want to follow Christ, we must follow the captain Christ has put over us, submitting to him "in all things." What does submission to a husband involve? Can a woman receive satisfaction in life if she adopts such a mind-set? Is she not betraying womanhood by capitulating to an outdated patriarchal system? Let's take a look at the goal and glory of a woman.

■ ■ ■

Discussion Questions

1. What parallels are there between the husband-wife and the Christ-church relationships?

2. How is the human relationship different from the spiritual relationship?

3. Is it wrong for a woman to serve in the military? Why? Why not?

4. Is it important to stand up for marriage in our society? Why? Why not?

5. Is Christian marriage threatened if our society opens marriage to homosexual couples or polygamists?

6. How has your marriage reflected the love of Christ to neighbors and friends?

7. The church looks to Christ to define her identity, her joy, and her activities. Is a wife defined by her husband in this way? If so, how? If not, why not?

8. How can a single woman relate to truths about marriage?

9. How can we help young men and women to rediscover the solidity and joy of Christian marriage?

10. Do you sometimes find it embarrassing to be loved? Why do you think this is the case? What can you do about it?

■ ■ ■

Resources

Boice, James Montgomery. *Foundations of the Christian Faith.* Downers Grove, Ill.: InterVarsity, 1986.

Bromiley, Geoffrey W. *God and Marriage.* Eugene, Ore.: Wipf and Stock, 1980.

Campbell, Ken M., ed. *Marriage and Family in the Biblical World.* Downers Grove, Ill.: InterVarsity, 2003.

Clowney, Edmund P. *The Church: Contours of Christian Theology,* ed., Gerald Bray. Downers Grove, Ill.: InterVarsity, 1995.

Grudem, Wayne and Dennis Rainey, eds. *Pastoral Leadership for Manhood and Womanhood.* Wheaton, Ill.: Crossway, 2002.

Well, someone tell me, when is it my turn?
Don't I get a dream for myself?
—FROM ROSE'S TURN

10

Glory

ON NATIONAL PUBLIC RADIO I heard the song called "Rose's Turn," from a musical written in 1959. The song is sung by a mother who has poured her life into making her daughter a success. When she realizes that her daughter no longer needs her, she agonizes over her own significance and stands on the empty stage at night, singing to no one. The song has a pounding, frenetic, petulant rhythm that sums up the cry of many women who desire a few moments of center stage fame:

> Well, someone tell me, when is it my turn?
> Don't I get a dream for myself?
> Starting now it's gonna be my turn. . . .
> Starting now I bat a thousand!
> This time, boys, I'm taking the bows and
> everything's coming up Rose!
> Everything's coming up roses
> this time for me!
> For me!![1]

What about glory? If Mary was the last woman to hope for the glory of bearing the Savior, how do women fit into God's plan now? Is being a wife and mother still the main goal of a woman, or has the death and resurrection of Jesus changed all that?

What Glory for Women?

Women who are stay-at-home moms or who have abandoned promising careers to follow a husband across the country can feel the tug of Rose's cry for glory. When my seven children were all young, my job was exhausting. Work days lasted eighteen hours or more, and I used to lock myself in the bathroom so I could think clearly enough to write my shopping list! Someone once gave me a cartoon drawing of a mom in the bathroom. Under the door, four or five sets of little fingers were inserted. Does a woman ever get out of the bathroom, the laundry room, and the kitchen to take a spot in the limelight? What kind of glory will she ever get if she makes a constant martyr of herself?

Standing on the stage, Rose is longing for someone to pay attention to her, to recognize her gifts, her efforts, her importance. She wants the lights to shine on her, for a change, and to feel the rush of success and recognition. The Bible does understand and respond to our need for glory, but it has a different notion of glory than the one Rose is seeking. A Christian woman knows that she is not put in this world to *stand in* the limelight, but to *be* the limelight—to shine the light of Christ into the darkness around her, shining that light on to others, lifting them up, encouraging them, drawing out their gifts. We are to be "concerned about the things of the Lord, so that [we] may be holy both in body and in spirit" (1 Cor. 7:34).

This is far from the spirit of our age which sees the fulfilled woman as strong, autonomous, and self-propelled. Feminists have taught us that "autonomy is what women's liberation is all about."[2] When I attended a women's college in the late sixties and early seventies, women were embarrassed to describe marriage and motherhood as a vocation. Since then, autonomy as a woman's ideal is no longer the sole domain of the radical left, but the common opinion of society at large. To describe a woman as in "submission" to her husband shocks most of us. These days, "submission" means sending an article to a magazine or registering a Web site on a search engine. Otherwise, only wimps submit.

Even Christian women sometimes choke on the apostle Paul's words: "Wives, submit to your husbands as to the Lord" (Eph. 5:22 NIV). They argue that Paul must mean "mutual" submission—wives and husbands submitting to each other out of love. One verse states this clearly, they reason. Paul says "Be filled with the Spirit. . . . submitting to one another in the fear of Christ" (Eph. 5:18, 21). This "submission-lite," by which each party simply considers the other's needs, can slip unnoticed past the politically correct guardians of our culture.

Christians *are* called to act selflessly and to lay down their own desires for those of their fellow believers. But Paul teaches in this passage that Christians have different ways of submitting. Some are called to be wives, some have masters to whom they must answer. And children are in a temporary state of submission to their parents until they grow up. To get the sense of Paul's instruction "submitting to one another," we must punctuate the verse with a colon. Paul is saying, "Submit to one another, and here's how." He shows the *ways* in which we submit: namely, wives to husbands, children to parents, servants to masters (or in our social structures, workers to bosses).[3]

If Paul were only teaching a general principle of mutual submission, why would he enumerate specific cases? If he had wanted to emphasize the mutuality of submission, he would have underlined *both* sides of the issue: "Slaves, submit to your masters, and masters to your slaves. Wives, submit to your husbands, and husbands to your wives. Children, submit to your parents, and parents to your children." He should even have said, "As the church submits to Christ, so Christ submits to the church."

The resurrection power and love of Christ infuses the authority structures with a Christian spirit, as we understand from other passages Paul has written. A husband will lead in a loving, sacrificial way. A parent will maintain authority over a child without stirring his heart to anger. A master will treat his slave as a brother in Christ. But such love does not destroy the structures. It would be foolish to argue that because some police officers misuse their authority, we should get rid of all police. It is not because some husbands misuse their authority in the home that we should destroy God's idea of family, with a father in charge.

Here we come to the crux of the issue. If a woman must submit to her husband, how can she not feel squashed? Aren't we past Paul's "patriarchal" ideas in the twenty-first century? Are we still to be bound by such an outdated model of marriage?

To answer these questions, we must look first at Paul's idea of submission and then at his notion of glory.

Submission

Paul often uses two principles which, if understood, help us see what submission looks like. The first is a principle I will call *radical positive obedience*. Paul describes this as *putting off and putting on*. I'll use some Bible texts here, so open a Bible and check me out, if you wish. When Paul talks about stealing (Eph. 4:28), he gives a simple command: "The thief must no longer steal." But he doesn't stop there. In order to conquer the sin of stealing, we must learn to work with our hands. But even this is not sufficient. The thief is to stop stealing and work, *in order to have something to give*. So the "negative" behavior is stealing. The "neutral," bridging behavior is working with your hands, and the "positive" behavior is generosity—giving away your belongings to others.

Paul applies the same principle to speech. It is not enough to stop lying (negative), or to be silent (neutral). We must speak the truth (positive) and thus build up those around us. He uses the same principle for drunkenness. We are not only to cease getting drunk (negative), but we are to be filled with the Spirit (neutral)[4] *so that* we can sing hymns and spiritual songs to encourage the church (positive).

The second principle is the *parallel principle.* Paul makes a specific parallel between Christ's relationship with the church and the husband's relationship to his wife, a relationship we began to explore in the last chapter. Spiritual-physical parallels in the Bible work both ways. What we know on the spiritual level teaches us about human experience and what we know of human experience helps us understand spiritual truth. When God created the profound physical and spiritual union experienced between a man and woman in marriage, He wanted to teach us about the relationship between Christ and the church. But as we learn of Christ and the church, we also learn a lot about our marriages. If we apply these two Pauline principles to submission, we will learn what radical positive submission looks like, and we will learn how a woman submits to her husband by seeing how the church is to submit to Christ.

From Negative to Positive

Women who rebel against their husband's authority, refusing to accept what God has placed in their lives for protection and for holiness, are obviously not in submission. You've seen this woman. Her husband cannot "make" her submit, so he becomes an appendage to her, useless as a husband and father. She takes everything into her own hands and makes him look like a fool in the process.

Radical positive obedience is just the opposite of this stubborn autonomy. It is not merely a grudging *passivity.* A wife doesn't just become silent and go into neutral. To obey Christ's command to submit, a wife must work actively to know and honor the heart desires of her husband. She conforms herself to its joys, its instincts, and its passions, and she encourages the children to do the same. Submitting to her husband is far more than avoiding the temptation to belittle him. It involves lifting him up, honoring him actively in her heart and before others, and verbally encouraging him. True submission in the sexual realm is not just letting him make love to her passive body. She is called to give of herself with joy. Not only should she avoid dominating her husband (see Gen. 3:16 and 4:7, where the meaning of dominating becomes clear), but she should desire to build his honor, whether in the eyes of neighbors, children, family members, or friends.

As Christ Loves the Church

We've seen how integrally related the spiritual and the physical are. God does not wipe away marriage after the resurrection, because it is the showpiece through which the world can have some idea of God's love for His people. A wife submits to her husband as the church submits to Christ. The church has a job description during its "fiancée" stage—from the time of her betrothal to God at the cross to the renewing of all things in the New Jerusalem, when there will no longer be any "marriage or giving in marriage." Her job is "to bring all things in heaven and on earth together under one head, even Christ" (Eph. 1:10 NIV).[5] As she does this, her Savior washes her and makes her holy (Eph. 5:26). The church, in her relation to Christ her husband brings every thought captive to Him (2 Cor. 10:5), has her thinking transformed by Him (Rom. 12:2) and conformed to His, and is washed clean by the water of His Word (Eph. 5:26). We could add a host of other things the church does to adopt Christ's heart.[6]

A "submissive" wife in the domain of her home has a job description parallel to that of the church in relation to Christ. The wife brings "all things" together under her husband's headship. Submission is not just letting your husband have the last word when you can't agree. It is more than letting him make decisions without objecting. Submission is actively gathering, ordering, and submitting to your husband's control all those things that are under your supervision (including the checkbook and the children).

I have been married for many years. As I gradually understand how radical the demands of true Christian submission are, I also realize how sinfully stubborn I am. I still sometimes resent the constraints of pleasing a human husband, thinking I know better and judging his decisions to be foolish. What pride and disdain can fill me, as I erect my own mind as the measure of all things! I have even less excuse for such thinking than some might have, because I am married to a godly man whose heart's desire is to serve his Savior. Even in the grace-filled marriage God has given me, I rebel.

Without the power and grace of Christ, the church cannot "bring all things together" under His headship. Without the power and grace of Christ, I will never begin to bring all things in my home together under the headship of my husband. That's why we have to be filled with the Spirit's power in order to submit. That's why women were included in the outpouring of the Spirit at Pentecost. They need the Spirit's strength and resurrection power to enable them to fulfill their calling as women. Part of that calling for those who are married is submission to a sinful, human husband. Submission is not for weaklings. It takes tremendous strength, as Jesus shows us when He submits to His Father's will and goes to the cross.

In my weakness I learn of Christ's strength, and I work at submitting to my husband, at coming in line with his heart, even when I don't understand it. As I obey my husband, I am also obeying Christ who has asked me to submit myself to a particular man, Peter Jones. As I do this, I am helping to bring all things together under Christ, since the man is the head of the woman and Christ is the head of the man. One day, when all things have been brought under Christ's control, He will lay them at the feet of the Father, to whom He submits (1 Cor. 15:21–28).

So what is submission for me as a wife? It is not mindless, wimpish passivity. It is a wholehearted participation in bringing glory to Christ by exalting the husband whom God has given me. I lift him up and honor him under Christ. God gave Peter to me and to our children to bring our family and home under the headship of Christ, which speaks the gospel in a world of confusion and instability. As children submit to their parents in the strength of the Lord; as employees or slaves submit to the wills of even their wicked bosses through the amazing power of the gospel; as wives submit without fear even to unbelieving husbands, we all grow up together into Him who is the head—Christ (Eph. 4:15)—and fill the whole universe with the knowledge of the glorious God of the gospel (Eph. 4:10).

I don't think we realize what a powerful effect such submission has. Christian women who throw themselves body and soul into the glorious task God has given them will bring honor to the name of the gospel, on earth and before the authorities in the heavenlies, both good and wicked. Do you begin to see what a privilege we have? Submission is a high calling, as our selfless Savior knew.

We do not have the time to examine all the practicalities of submission. God places women in extremely difficult situations sometimes, and we are called to exercise great discernment as we "prove out" the will of God. Submission is never easy! It requires all that we are—our minds, our wills, our wisdom, our bodies. But God has given us a wealth of information in His Word. He has given us a soft and tender heart that desires to please Him. He has given us the power and joy of the Spirit that allows us to see meaning in circumstances that would spell depression for others.

If you are suffering in your situation as a woman and you are a believer, don't forget that God fields His strongest heroes against the toughest teams. God is calling you to express the gospel in the reality of your difficulties. He will be honored as you prove out His will and one day, even if no one else ever says it to you, you will hear from your dear Savior's mouth those precious and refreshing words, "Well done . . . Enter into the joy of your master" (Matt. 25:23 ESV). When we act this way, bringing glory not to ourselves but to our Creator, our friends and neighbors are intrigued by the God we serve and end up praising and honoring Him too: "Conduct yourselves honorably among the Gentiles, so that in a case where they speak against you as those who do evil, they may, by observing your good works, glorify God in a day of visitation" (1 Pet. 2:12).

Glory

There *is* glory to be had in the Christian life, and women get their share, for as we submit and give glory to those in authority over us, the glory comes showering back down on us.

Man Glorifies God, but God Glorifies Man

The man is the "image and glory of God," says Paul. How astounding that God defines man as "the glory of God." This is the highest honor he could be given. God expects man to glorify Him, but He also calls man His glory. There is a reciprocal "glorification" process here. Man's purpose in life is "to glorify God and enjoy Him forever."[7] But God pours out glory on the man, by creating him in His image, by calling him into service, by setting His love on him, by rescuing him from his state of hopelessness, and by re-creating him in the image not only of God, but as a new man in the image of Jesus Christ.

In 1 Corinthians 11, Paul emphasizes the man as male. All humans are in some sense the "glory of God," created in His image, but God calls the male to a special representative glory. Adam the male, is the first to be created. On him God's glory rests before the woman exists. And so man (male) is the glory of God in a different way than man (female). Adam, in his representative role, glorifies His Savior by being male. This maleness, a part of Adam's identity as God's image, is the "glory of God." We cannot say that Adam is the sum of the glory of God. That role is reserved for an *adam* (the Hebrew word for "man"), but not for the first *adam*. It is reserved for Adam's son Christ, a human male, God incarnate, who is the "radiance of [God's] glory, the exact expression of His nature" (Heb. 1:3).

The Woman Glorifies the Man, but the Man Glorifies the Woman

Paul tells us that the man is the *image and glory* of God and that the woman is the *glory* of the man, though not the *image* of the man. Woman is made in *God's* image, not in the image of the man. However, she is the *glory* of the man, created in a particular place for a particular reason. Eve is created to be a helper to Adam. She is suited to him (Gen. 2:23), and he revels in her beauty. She is just right, just what he is looking for, just what he needs—"bone of my bone, and flesh of my flesh." She is a kind of crown to humanity, the most beautiful creation of God, which He saves for the end, as the grand finale of creation.

From the time I was a little girl, I was far more interested in books than makeup, in theology than clothes. It has been a struggle for me to understand that reveling in my physical beauty (such as it is!) honors my husband and my Creator. I have tried, with only painstaking progress, to put into practice what I believe in my head: that a woman is meant to stimulate a "Wow" reaction in a man. God presents Eve to Adam as a great and wondrous birthday surprise. After he finishes "unwrapping" all the gifts God has given him, absorbing the warmth of the sun's rays, delighting in the fragrance of a gardenia, admiring the splendid strength of an ox, he has found no creature like him with whom he can have true fellowship. Then God knocks him flat (so that he cannot boast in any good work) and presents him with the most stunningly beautiful creature in all creation, a woman who is to be his glory. Adam needs no lessons. His breath is taken away when he sees Eve, for her beauty is accessible, personal, human, intimate, and verbal.

Like Adam, a godly man sees his wife as his glory, rejoicing in body and soul at the miraculous combination of physical beauty, wisdom, brains, speech, abilities, strength, and joy. When we speak of a woman as man's glory, we must not think "trophy wife." A man is not to use the woman for his own glory. Nor is the woman to use her glorious sexuality to manipulate and control her husband. He remains her "head," just as Christ is the "head" of the man: "But I want you to understand that the head of every man is Christ, the head of a wife is her husband, and the head of Christ is God" (1 Cor. 11:3 ESV).

The authority of a husband over his wife is so clear in the Scriptures that those who disagree must go to all kinds of lengths to read against the plain meaning of the texts. There is no getting around the fact that the Bible places the husband squarely in authority in his home as it also places men in authority in the church. Paul states these themes clearly in 1 Corinthians 11, as well as in other passages and he uses them to draw practical implications: "[The man] is God's image and glory, but woman is man's glory. For man did not come from woman, but woman came from man; and man was not created for woman, but woman for man. This is why a woman should have [a symbol of] authority on her head, because of the angels."[8]

Paul instructs women to behave in certain ways both at home and in the church because of the principles he lays down. He argues that the creation goal for the first woman, Eve, is reflected in the fact that she was taken from Adam, the man, and was created for him. A married woman serves God by serving her husband as God intended. She is to respect her husband (Eph. 5:33; 1 Pet. 3:2), to call him "lord" (1 Pet. 3:6), to love him (Titus 2:4), to obey him (1 Pet. 3:6), not holding her body back from him sexually (1 Cor. 7:4). She is to love their children and to spend her time in busy service of the household (1 Tim. 5:10). She is not to spend her time in everyone else's home, telling them what to do (1 Tim. 5:13). She is not to gossip or drink too much (1 Tim. 5:13), but is to have a quiet and reverent spirit (Titus 2:3; 1 Pet. 3:4; 1 Tim. 2:12), eager to help in the church, to show hospitality and to do all kinds of good works (1 Tim. 5:10).

Wise women who have learned to put these things into practice are to teach other women how to love their husbands, to pour their energies into their own homes and children, and to become like the women of the Old Testament who showed their respect to their husbands and didn't give way to fear.

Radical stuff. Biblical stuff.

We Christian women need to live our glory boldly in a culture that understands so little of the true character of women. We need not fear to live and to speak these truths. Recently I was standing in line at the grocery store, chatting with the cashier. I mentioned how fortunate I was that my husband had provided for me so faithfully and that though he earns the money, he trusts me implicitly to spend it for the good of the home. The man behind me piped up, "Women are always griping. I never thought I'd ever hear a woman praise her husband. Ya gotta love it!"

My simple gratitude for my husband's care encouraged this man. How easy it is for us as women to profit from our place of glory to belittle and tear down our husbands. God calls us to use our feminine glory to build them up, not tear them down. Part of a woman's worship of God is to honor and respect her husband. These sound, undeniable biblical truths have come to be seen as radical and dangerous. A woman who believes that she is under her husband's authority is seen as a "radical fundamentalist," a danger to democracy and to the stability of the world. The gospel of feminism compels today's liberated women to rescue women under the shackles of such an authority system. Christian submission is compared to the worst of Taliban excesses.

Christian women are not oppressed slaves, and we need to stop feeling so sorry for ourselves! I know some women *are* oppressed, and the church needs to be the first to rush to their aid. But many Christian women suffer not because their husbands are being too macho, but because their husbands are too sinful, lazy, or selfish to take godly leadership in the home. Women whose Christian husbands exercise leadership receive glory while offering respect.

A Christian woman receives a torrent of glory. As the saying goes, "What goes up must come down." A Christian woman offers respect, obedience, trust, and confidence to her husband. In return, she receives glory poured out on her head like an anointing oil that starts in heaven and runs first onto the head of Christ the high priest, then onto the head of her human authority (her husband) and finally onto her own head. She receives glory from God for her obedience and faith, but she also receives the honor and glory of her husband.

How many times have people had to put up with my husband singing my praises? I hate to imagine! I'm far from a perfect wife, but as I have tried by God's power and grace to submit to my husband, to attune my heart to his desires, to uphold him in his service to Christ—I have received over and over the expression of his direct thanks, the words of praise that well up from his heart in my honor as he expresses his gratitude to God for my place in his life.

Proverbs 31 shows us the picture of the faithful wife rewarded by the praise of her husband and children: "Her sons rise up and call her blessed. Her husband also praises her: 'Many women are capable, but you surpass them all!'" (Prov. 31:28–29). A woman who honors the Lord receives the praise of her children, her husband, her church, and most of all, her Savior! What more recognition could she want?

Jesus Glorifies God, but God Lifts Him Up in Glory

In his discussion of the relationship between a man and his wife, Paul ties marriage to the Trinity. God sets all His glory in Jesus Christ, who is the exact representation of the living God (Col. 1:15, 20; Heb. 1:3). The glory given to Christ by the Father shines through Jesus into our hearts, where it shines forth: "For God, who said, 'Let light shine out of darkness,' has shone in our hearts to give the light of the knowledge of the glory of God in the face of Jesus Christ" (2 Cor. 4:6 ESV).

Just as the woman glorifies the man and is glorified by the man, so Jesus glorifies the Father, and is glorified by the Father. The Son glorifies the Father in submission to Him; the man glorifies Christ in submission to Him; and a wife glorifies her husband in submission to him.

We clearly see submission in Christ's relationship to the Father. Christ emphasizes His dependence on the Father, and the constraint to "be about [His] Father's business." He must accomplish the calling for which the Father has sent Him into the world. Some argue that Jesus is only in submission to the Father during His time on earth, but this seems doubtful in light of what Paul says:

> Then comes the end, when he delivers the kingdom to God
> the Father after destroying every rule and every authority
> and power. For he must reign until he has put all his enemies
> under his feet. The last enemy to be destroyed is death. For
> "God has put all things in subjection under his feet." But
> when it says, "all things are put in subjection," it is plain that
> he is excepted who put all things in subjection under him.
> When all things are subjected to him, then the Son himself
> will also be subjected to him who put all things in subjection
> under him, that God may be all in all (1 Cor. 15:24–28 ESV).

It is clear in this passage that Jesus Christ submits to the Father after He has accomplished all that God asked Him to do. When the church, by the power of the Holy Spirit, has finished its job of bringing everything under Christ's headship, Christ will present it all to the Father. The Father is not subject to Christ, but vice versa. Other Scriptures support the notion that God the Son is in submission to the Father. He was present with the Father, delighting in creation and participated in that creation. He was the Word with God, but was also God (John 1:1). Christ is both eternally obedient to the Father and eternally equal to the Father. "Make your own attitude that of Christ Jesus, who, existing in the form of God, did not consider equality with God as something to be used for His own advantage" (Phil. 2:5–6.)

Christ's submission to the Father in no way demeans Him or makes Him less important, less valuable—a second-class member of the Trinity. The Holy Spirit also, in full unity and equality with both the Father and the Son, serves both the Father and the Son. Jesus has the authority to send the Spirit, whose job it is to bring glory to Christ. The three persons of the Trinity are in perfect union, perfect communion, and yet they are distinguishable and have different "roles," if such a word can be used for such a mysterious subject.

Why do I muddle through such an abstract idea as the Trinity? The church has grappled with these issues for centuries. Entire councils have met, disagreed, ended in church splits, and continued the debate until our own day. I don't have as good a grasp on these issues as the many knowledgeable theologians who have studied them for years. But the women's issue is tied directly to the Trinity by Paul, so there is no way to avoid linking these two ideas. In addition, reflection on the Trinity sheds wonderful light on the relationship between a husband and a wife.

Christ submits Himself to the Father's will, which means He leaves heaven to embody on earth the stunning, dangerous glory of God. That glory is veiled in a Jewish baby, born in the shadows of a winter evening, surrounded by the stench of donkey's dung. It is further veiled as Christ is mocked, scorned, ignored, hated, and murdered. Even when it bursts forth from the earth and when its true nature is revealed by the fact that death could not shackle it, that glory is not fully received, understood, or seen. The glory of Christ will only be seen fully when His work is completed, when the church will have manifested it over time, through suffering, in a world still groaning under the burden of sin.

The glory of Christ is now seen by the world through the church and through families who infuse God's created structures with the love and power of the resurrected Christ. The resurrection is Christ's stamp of approval from God the Father. The Jesus who returns from the grave is the first new man. But the will of the Father is that Christ should father countless children, as the Spirit hovers over the union of Christ and the church, engendering many newborn children for the Kingdom. The Spirit glorifies Christ in the church until the final return of Christ as Judge. God *will* glorify the Son. His brilliance will one day shine over the entire earth so that every man, woman, and child will, whether by force or with a good heart, bow down to acknowledge His kingship. The submission that the Son offers to the Father results in glory that comes pouring back down the ladder.

The Father lifts up the Son and glorifies Him, raising Him from earth back to heaven and setting all things in heaven and on earth under His feet. Jesus bestows glory on the man, renewing and strengthening him to represent Him on earth. The man who was originally set in the garden as viceroy regains his position through the power of Christ as He is re-created by the resurrection. In the New Testament, the man does not lose his authority in the home, but infuses that authority with a new grace and power, since he is now living in the Spirit of the resurrected Christ. He keeps his position of responsibility in his home and in the church, since God still respects His creation structures.

There is some mysterious sense in which the male stands, head bared, in the presence of Christ, reporting directly, without any other "authority" on his head. He wears no head covering to symbolize submission to another human authority. He enters directly into the presence of Christ and answers to Him. He is the image and glory of God. As he obeys Christ in this role, Christ pours glory on his head.

Of course, Jesus also pours His glory on women, who are partakers of grace with men. In this sense, the glory Christ gives His church is no respecter of position, race, or gender. But a married woman relates to Christ in her role as wife as one "under authority." In her worship of Christ, a woman's submission to her husband is an occasion for honor and glory. Just as Jesus delights in doing His Father's will, just as the church delights in serving her husband Christ, so a married woman delights in serving Christ *by* serving her husband. In Christian service, she helps her husband to fill and have dominion over the earth.

Ultimate Fruitfulness

As we respect God's structures, we revel in the unity of love and communion that results from our obedience. We also relish the fruit of those structures. God made marriage to teach us of unity, but also to show us a picture of fruitful creativity. In this, too, we humans reflect God. God the Creator allows us to participate in the joy of creating. After my daughter gave birth recently, she exclaimed, "I can't believe you did this seven times, Mom!" But Jesus was right. A mother forgets the suffering of childbirth in the joy of holding her newborn baby (John 16:21).

Five of my seven children were born in a peaceful French clinic, where the delivery room had plate-glass windows looking out into the bright azure skies of Provence and the shimmering leaves of the ever-present plane trees. All the pain of birth was swept away in a triumphant cry, "It's finished!" A new life was beginning—a life God had given me the joy of helping to create and bring into the world. I can't explain the depth of satisfaction, joy, glory, and peace that I experienced in those first hours holding a new baby.

A mother and father witnessing the birth of their child echo what wisdom says as it stands by God watching and participating in creation, "delighting in the children of man" (Prov. 8:31 ESV). God makes and gives life, but allows us the joy of "creating" children by the sexual union of love. We receive children from His hand with great joy, "filling the earth" until God decides when our human "quiver" is full.

As we embrace fruitfulness, we remember that filling the earth is greater than the joyful task of physical reproduction. The ultimate marriage, between Christ and His bride, produces new creatures, of which the resurrected Jesus was the first example. Throughout history, mankind has longed for a truly new version of the human being. Nazi Germany dreamed of the *bermensche,* and today's new spirituality speaks of *homo noeticus* (new man). Christians have already met the unique superman, the true "new man." We know Him well. We are married to Him! United to the Bridegroom Jesus, His church, in everlasting fidelity, produces fruit to fill the universe. God has approved and honored the new man and has "put everything under His feet and appointed Him as head over everything for the church, which is His body, the fullness of the One who fills all things in every way" (Eph. 1:22–23).

Jesus, in His death, resurrection and ascension to heaven, covers all the territory: "The One who descended is the same as the One who ascended far above all the heavens, that He might fill all things" (Eph. 4:10). Do you shiver with fear when you see the strange red earth of Mars or the unimaginably distant beauty of the nebulae as shown by the Hubble telescope? Jesus has been there. He has not only created, but has personally explored the realms of the universe and has brought them under His control. And this Jesus is our Bridegroom, who will one day carry us over the threshold of death and take us to the glorious home He has been getting ready for us.

It is by His Spirit that we are enabled as Christians to see the fruit of new birth in the hearts of our friends and neighbors. It is the triumphant fruit of our marriage with Him that will be seen on the last day, when He comes to judge the world and will welcome to the wedding feast all those who have by faith been made children of God. In Christ, our goal is not *only* to produce physical children, but to produce spiritual children, among whom, by God's grace are our physical children. The hovering, creative power of the Spirit that first brought life out of chaos at creation "produces fruit" for the gospel until the whole earth is filled with the knowledge of Christ as the waters fill the seas.

As we see the richness of the relationship between Christ and His church and as we see the parallels the Bible makes between this marriage and human marriage, we begin to understand why marriage is such a holy arrangement. The very structure was created so that we would be able to understand something of the greater spiritual relationship. As Christians, we must honor that marriage relationship in our own lives and stand up for it in public.

Christian women need to be fans not only of their husbands, but of men in general. Christian men need to honor their own sexuality and the "set apartness" of their seed. Our entire sexual and family life is informed by the truths of the gospel. God has given us a rich understanding of marriage and sexuality, and He expects us to be thinking through personal and practical issues on the basis of such an understanding.

A new social model of very unholy marriage prevails, but we need not fear. God holds Christian marriages in honor. If we call to Him, He is able and willing to help us. In our immediate future, society will so tamper with sexuality that "marriage" will no longer hold its Christian intent. Christians will be scorned for holding to an outdated, oppressive social structure. Christians who hold to the submission of a wife to her husband will be hated and perhaps prosecuted. We must hold our heads high, however, affirming the beauty of sexuality and marriage and rejoicing in its power to show the astounding love relationship between

Jesus and His perfect bride, the church. It is because we understand the nature of that relationship that we live our Christian marriages with fierce dedication to God's principles.

■ ■ ■

Discussion Questions

1. To what human beings do you owe submission? In what areas? How is this difficult? How is it rewarding?

2. To whom did Jesus owe allegiance and conform His will?

3. If you are married, is there any limit to your submission to your husband? Is there ever a time when you should not conform your will to his?

4. Whose praise do you most value, humanly speaking? How do you keep your focus on God's praise, rather than on the praise of people? Do these dovetail sometimes?

5. How can you be your husband's glory? God's glory?

6. Over whom do you have authority? Do you look for ways of glorifying those under your authority? How might you do this?

7. In your own life, define the attitudes and actions that would lead you from active rebellion to active obedience. What is the "neutral" behavior?

8. If you are married, how can you "bring all things" under the headship of your husband in the home? What is the hardest thing about this?

9. How can you as a woman help to bring all things under Christ's headship in your church?

10. If you are single, where do you fit on the "glory ladder"?

■ ■ ■

Resources

Dillow, Linda and Lorraine Pintus. *Intimate Issues: Conversations Woman to Woman*. New York: Waterbrook Press, 1999.

Doriani, Dan. *Women and Ministry: What the Bible Teaches*. Wheaton, Ill.: Crossway, 2003.

Hove, Richard. *Equality in Christ: Galatians 3:28 and the Gender Dispute*. Wheaton, Ill.: Crossway, 1999.

House, Wayne. *The Role of Women in Ministry Today*. Nashville: Thomas Nelson, 1990.

Hunt, Susan and Barbara Thompson. *The Legacy of Biblical Womanhood*. Wheaton, Ill.: Crossway, 2003.

LaHaye, Beverly and Janice Shaw Crouse. *A Different Kind of Strength: Rediscovering the Power of Being a Woman*. Eugene, Ore.: Harvest House, 2001.

Patterson, Dorothy Kelley. *Where's Mom?* Wheaton, Ill.: Crossway, 2003.

Saucy, Robert and Judith K. Ten Elsof, eds. *Women and Men in Ministry: A Complementary Perspective*. Chicago: Moody, 2001

Ware, Bruce. *Summaries of the Egalitarian and Complementarian Positions on the Role of Women in the Home and in Christian Ministry*. Booklet, available at www.cbmw.org.

Throughout the millennia of human history, . . . people took for granted that the differences between men and women were so obvious as to need no comment. They accepted the way things were. But our easy assumptions have been assailed and confused; we have lost our bearings in a fog of rhetoric about something called equality, so that I find myself in the uncomfortable position of having to belabor to educated people what was once perfectly obvious to the simplest peasant.

—ELISABETH ELLIOT

11
■■■■■

Squashed?

ONE MORNING, OUR FRIEND Gerry was on his usual 5:00 a.m. bike ride. He may have been praying for the three little girls he and his wife Lori recently adopted. Out of nowhere, a car came whizzing by, hitting Gerry and dragging the bike a mile down the road. Gerry was left for dead by the side of the road. In a recent e-mail to friends and family, Lori writes of Gerry's progress as he slowly emerges from a coma: "Today I received exciting news! About 4:00 a.m. this morning, Gerry lifted his head, back and raised up on his elbows, attempting to swing his leg around like he was trying to get up out of bed." After more details, Lori asks for prayer for a friend, and then adds: "May the Lord be as close to her and her family as he has been to me (and I know Gerry) during our time of need. Rejoice in the Lord always, again I say Rejoice! (Phil. 4:4)."

How is it that Lori, watching the senseless agony of her kind, godly husband, can rejoice in the Lord and commend Him to others? Did Lori get what she wants from life?

No and yes. If you are not yet a member of God's family, you may not understand how Lori can be satisfied with life in the middle of so much pain. But Lori's attitude shows why Christian women really do have it all. I don't mean this in any superficial way, because in the Christian woman's life, joy, satisfaction, and glory are often found in suffering, giving up, letting go, and sacrificing for others.

How these things can be satisfying is mysterious. But we all admire Lori's heroism, though she would not see it as such herself. Beneath our claim to rights, we understand that the greater good is often served by self-sacrifice.

Christian women find satisfaction in all five areas mentioned at the beginning of the book. They discover satisfying relationships with both men and women, a place to call home, children, and eternal significance.

Christian Men Treat Women with Respect

Christian women belong to a church family in which they have unusually deep and satisfying relationships. Since we joined our 250-member church in 1994, it has experienced ten cancer deaths, three deaths of older members, and four serious cancer cases in younger members who are, for the moment, winning the battle. Several other members have had major medical problems or lost children to miscarriage or birth defects (among them our own grandson Jonathan). This high incidence of suffering has drawn us very close.

At our last thanksgiving service, due to a problem with our roving microphone, members had to walk up front to express their thanks to the Lord. Marsha, a recent widow of a faithful elder, wanted to speak. She whispered something in our pastor's ear, to which he gave a smile, a nod, and an extended arm. Marsha clung to that arm for courage and support as she spoke. Then her mother got up to speak and she, too, clung to the pastor's arm. Next, up came the pastor's own eighteen-year-old daughter. He laughed and said, "I don't suppose *you* need my arm!" But she responded, with a gorgeous smile, "I'd love to hold your arm, Daddy," and she did, throughout her honest and lovely testimony of how God had changed her heart when she had resisted moving to Escondido, where her father had been called as pastor.

This is the reality of my church life. The male elders who minister to us are men we trust. We rely on them for help, turn to them for advice, and speak our minds about issues that trouble us. I have seen the generosity and self-sacrifice of the male leaders in our church and have experienced their care not only for me and for my family, but for the women in our church. They are there for the widows, for the sick, and for those with marriage difficulties or addictions. They give of their time, their means, and their emotional support to provide whatever they can to any member of the church.

Men and women trust one another. We pray together, weep together, eat and sing together. The leadership encourages the women in several ways. They pray regularly and publicly for our work in the church and for women who are or who would like to be pregnant. They provide the financial resources to accomplish our women's ministry. They stay abreast of our decisions by appointing an elder to sit in on our monthly women's organizational meeting, thus coordinating our work with that of the entire church. The president of our women's council attends the public portion of the session meeting in order to understand the direction of church policies. Women are active on church committees, in outreach to the community, in mercy ministries, and in the teaching of our children. We organize specific ministry for women by women, in obedience to the Bible's commands for older women to encourage and teach younger women.

Some structures outside of church life may provide emotional closeness, but they are unified by some common cause or social class. The deep friendship extended to members of our church transcends cultural and economic boundaries. Where but in a church will well-to-do businessmen relate to ex-drug addicts, a single woman rejoice for newlyweds, a public school teacher encourage homeschool families, a couple married for fifty years pray for those on the edge of divorce? We're not as integrated as we will one day be in heaven, but we're learning that we are *all* "more sinful, evil, and weak than we ever dared imagine, yet more valued, accepted, and loved than we ever dared hope." In Christ, no ethnic, gender, or societal barriers can remain, since we are all forgiven sinners.

The genuinely respectful relationships that women would love to have with men *really do happen* in the body of Christ. I'm tired of hearing people dump on the church. Christians are not perfect, but I've been a member of seven different churches over the last half century and have seen, on the whole, wonderfully healthy, respectful relationships between men and women. Fathers can show affection to their daughters without falling into abuse. Brothers and sisters can have truly deep relationships because each is striving to be selfless and to please Christ. Wives respect and love their husbands not only because they are commanded to by their Savior, but also because their husbands are loving them as Christ loved His church (or at least trying!), sacrificing their lives for their wives to protect and honor them, building them up, and encouraging the use of their gifts.

The atmosphere in which a Christian woman develops in the church is the safest and most freeing atmosphere possible. I realize that some churches do not provide an encouraging atmosphere for women. Some churches, desirous of respecting the differences between men and women, come to odd, unbiblical conclusions. One church debated whether women should contribute to an e-mail discussion! One refused to sing hymns written by women. (I wonder what they do with Mary's song in Luke 1.)

Christian husbands also can abuse the authority given them by Christ and "lord it over" their wives, but do not accuse "Christianity" or Christ Himself for the abuses of some Christians. A church that understands the gospel will admire and respect the wisdom and godliness of its women. A man who understands the gospel *cannot* "lord it over" anyone, especially his wife, who is his own flesh. "Christian" men who misuse their position will one day answer to the perfect man, the head of the church. I only hope when they meet Christ, that He will not say, "Depart from Me, you who are cursed" (Matt. 25:41). Such is the risk for a man who blasphemes the name of Christ by calling himself a Christian and dishonoring the woman Christ has placed in his care.

The Christian men I know treat their wives as precious treasures. They dote on them, admire them, depend on them, rejoice in them, cherish them, praise them, and sacrifice for them. This is as it should be. Are they perfect? Of course not. Men have lots to learn about how to listen, how to honor and use women's gifts, and how to show women they care. But Christian women have a lot to learn about honoring men, admiring them, understanding their male version of godliness, and comforting them when they fear.

Christ Helps Women Relate to Men

Both men and women need an outside source of power from which to draw the strength for healthy relationships. The Christian faith provides the miraculous power necessary for Christian couples to avoid being sucked into the destructive vortex of a bad relationship. The gospel transforms a woman's heart in three ways that allow her to relate with grace and power to her husband and children.

Peace

A Christian woman is in subjection not ultimately to her husband but to Christ, so she need not fear. By His Spirit, Christ gives a woman the faith to trust men, who are not inherently trustworthy. The Christian woman is at *peace* because she trusts in God, who is totally reliable, perfectly loving, and all-powerful.

In his letter to a suffering Christian church, the apostle Peter speaks specifically to women under the authority of unbelieving husbands. Such women have little reason to trust their husbands, who are not in submission to the gospel. Even to such women, however, Peter gives the following advice: "Submit yourselves to your own husbands so that, even if some disobey the [Christian] message, they may be won over without a message by the way their wives live, when they observe your pure, reverent lives . . . For in the past, the holy women who hoped in God also beautified themselves in this way, submitting to their own husbands, just as Sarah obeyed Abraham, calling him lord. You have become her children when you do good and aren't frightened by anything alarming" (1 Pet. 3:1–2, 5–6).

Sarah obeyed Abraham even when he exposed her to the risk of adultery in order to save his own life. Peter does not condone Abraham's behavior, but was aware of the incident as he writes of Sarah's faith. God watches over a woman even when her husband is making bad decisions. She cannot always trust her husband's instincts, but she *can* trust God's care. This steady faith in the goodness of God is what takes the fear out of a Christian woman's heart, even when she suffers unjustly. This faith allowed our friend Yvette not to fear her husband, though she never knew what he would do next. Her peace was a shining testimony of her faith in God, both to her husband and to all who knew her.[1]

Power

Secondly, a Christian woman receives *power* from Christ for submission. It takes a strong person to submit to authority, whether in the workplace, in the army, in school, or in a marriage. In marriage a woman is at her most vulnerable and submission is, therefore, the most difficult. Marriage is where you can be most easily hurt, where the wounds go deepest, where you have the least power. But Christ went through more humiliation and gave up more "rights" than any married woman. I sound illogical, talking about suffering when I've just said that wives are well-treated by Christian husbands. However, some women live with unbelievers and some with very "unchristian" Christian men. All women experience suffering of some kind in their relationships with their husbands.

It takes God's power to lay down our rights. Rearing seven children taught me very early in my marriage that I had no "rights." When I gave up my rights, I was a much happier mother and wife! One night, after midnight, I had to call on a doctor in our French village. This bleary-eyed man answered in a foul mood.

"This is the second night my sleep has been disturbed!" he growled.

I wanted to answer, "Sir, I have not had a full night's sleep in about four and one-half years. You chose to be a doctor. I chose to be a mother. Get over it!"

Fortunately, the Lord gave me the grace not to say anything.

Our true power as Christian women is to be like Christ, whose job was not defined by self-fulfillment, rights, or career advancement. Those who seek such goals may achieve them, but, as Jesus said, "they have their reward." If we want more than the vain glory our world has to offer, we must answer the call to glory issued by Christ. Our call is to love Him and do what He asks us, wherever He sets us, as willingly as we can, by relying on his grace and humility.

Whether you are a mother of twelve or a single woman; whether you are deprived of the use of your body or a star athlete; whether you live in a shack or a mansion; you are called to the same calling—to love and obey Christ in the joy of your salvation. This is why a Christian woman does not slave away in a continual haze of guilt. She is not squashed, since she is forever loved and valued by the living God and her service to others is her service of joy and praise to her Creator and Savior.

A Tender Heart

The third gift God gives us is a soft heart. To love a man, a woman's heart must be made fit. It is hard to love men, because we are so unlike them. I often want to scold my husband for not acting as he "should." But my arrogant self-righteousness will not strengthen our marriage. Christ strengthens it by patiently softening my heart and that of my husband.

When I was a little girl, I would sometimes have enough money from collecting and redeeming empty soda bottles to buy myself a soda at Bert and Tom's delicatessen. I would shove the paper on my straw down until it was a hard little accordion on the counter. Then I would let one drop of soda fall on it and watch that squashed worm of paper writhe, grow, wriggle, and stretch. That little dry paper reminds me of my heart—all dry and wrinkled up. But as Christ's blood drops on to my shriveled heart, it begins to soften, to move, to grow. It comes alive. I receive a heart of compassion instead of hatred, of "flesh" instead of "stone."

This soft heart enables the Christian woman to have satisfying relationships with her husband. No matter how unloving or selfish he may be, she will be empowered to follow him without fear, to submit to him through the power of Christ, and to love him with a tender heart. In so doing she is following, submitting to, and loving her faithful heavenly husband.

Meaningful Relations with Women

The same spiritual principles apply to our relationships with women. The Christian woman is at peace with other women because her identity is safe in Christ. She has power to submit to women in positions of authority over her, and to love women who are her natural enemies. Christian women have tender hearts, and they nurture one another within the Christian family. The close, natural relationships Christian women have infuses peace, strength, and compassion into the family of God.

Reflecting on woman-to-woman relationships leads us to consider the cultural context in which we live. When we returned to the United States in 1985 for a brief furlough, we put our children in American schools. Myriam, our first-grader, trotted off happily to school and was unaware of the humiliation of being put in with the "cupcakes" because she couldn't yet read in English (only in French). But the "cupcakes" were not the worst of it. One day she was punished for holding hands with another six-year-old girl! How had the American culture come to fear lesbian tendencies in such an innocent gesture?

That was 1985. Such overtones are now omnipresent. Our newspaper this morning had a full-spread picture of two women holding each other at the waist and staring longingly into each other's eyes. Six thousand gay and lesbian couples obtained marriage certificates from a renegade city hall in San Francisco, and thousands more have become legally married in Massachusetts. The battle to defend marriage in America is all but lost, without miraculous intervention from God.

Unfortunately, the disintegration of sex as God intended it has destroyed normal interaction between close women friends. When I was in high school, my Latin teacher and my previous fourth-grade teacher, both Christians, lived together. No one thought they were lesbians, and they weren't! They were good friends who found it efficient to share expenses. Now, unfortunately, such innocent arrangements are immediately suspect.

Christian Women Have Strong Friendships

In the Christian church, woman-to-woman friendships can be marvelous and deep, without lesbian overtones.[2] Christian women in stable, sound marriages are free to create strong relationships with other women. They express affection without fear and extend comfort and care in sister-to-sister or mother-to-daughter relationships. The Bible encourages such strong relationships, requiring Christian women to instruct and nurture one another: "Older women are ... to teach what is good, so that they may encourage the young women to love their husbands and children, to be sensible, pure, good homemakers, and submissive to their husbands, so that God's message will not be slandered" (Titus 2:3–5).

Such friendships do not tear down marriages or serve as gossip centers. Christian women do not use their meetings to tear one another down or destroy the church. They seek prayer and advice in order to show more love to their families and to the members of their church. Their relationships do not threaten but strengthen their marriages and families.

I have been meeting for prayer each week with a group of four women for over seven years now. We are honest within the bounds of respect to our husbands and children, and we always leave encouraged to love them more. We don't come away hardened in sinful attitudes toward family or church members, whatever the reason for our initial annoyance. Our precious friendship spurs us to good works, humility, love, hope, and courage. We watch in delight as God answers our prayers, keeping our children in His hand through thick and thin.

A Christian woman's relationship with her own daughter and mother are also transformed by the power of the gospel. Human frictions exist in every mother-daughter relationship, but the Christian gospel brings truth to bear from the outside. A daughter who loves Christ realizes that she need not be exactly like (or unlike) her mother, because her identity is in Christ. From that peaceful place, she can even counsel her own mother. I have five godly, warm, loving, wise, and wonderful daughters, whose love and advice I treasure. (I also have two great sons!) I have no desire at all to sing Rose's song: "Don't I get a dream for myself?" My daughters are a dream come true for me, as is my loving daughter-in-law. I delight most in seeing them follow the Lord, pouring out their lives in service to Christ and in love to those around them.

What may look like a life of self-denial has given me deep satisfaction. I didn't waste a good college education or miss a promising career. Even those women who wade through the deepest, darkest waters of suffering (which I have *not* experienced) become refreshing springs under the loving hand of Jesus. A Christian woman's place is where God puts her. There she thrives. There she is at home.

A Place to Call Home

When we had been in France for about two years, we discovered that our daughter was profoundly deaf. I made a trip to the United States to research our educational possibilities. On my way back, in the bubble of the airplane, where time stands still and space has no meaning, I pondered my place in the world. America was no longer home, but neither was France, especially now that we had a deaf child. Which language should she learn? Should she speak English and not communicate with her neighbors? Should she speak French and not communicate with her grandparents? Could she possibly learn two?

I did not understand why God would put us in France, then give our family a language-dependent handicap. Deafness seemed to work against God's calling. In that timeless bubble, I suddenly understood that I was a citizen of Christ's country. He was my King, and He determined the laws under which I was to live. He alone had the power to make my house into His home. If He had given us a deaf child in a bilingual situation, He would work things out for our good and His glory.

Now that our deaf daughter is an adult, I see how miraculously God met all our needs. He gave Gabrielle a good mind and a hardworking nature. He led us to a method of communication called Cued Speech, which not only gave her access to both English and French, but gave her the linguistic foundation to go on and learn Spanish, German, Russian, Greek, Hebrew, and several sign languages. Along with the trial, He gave strength to get through and a torrent of blessings.

Christian Women Carry Their Home with Them

All Christians find their home in Christ, not in human relationships or cultural habits. God sets us in families, and we appreciate a restful home. Women enjoy creating cozy places for ourselves and our families, but until we understand that Jesus is our home, we cannot be free to analyze, evaluate, and sort out our priorities and our choices. Where should we live? What is important to us? How are we to relate to our things, our furniture, our cars, our activities? A Christian woman can afford to be courageous, because she need not depend on the safety of a physical home. She depends on the only safe home God has promised her—His arms.

Christian women are like turtles, able to carry our home around with us. Home does not depend on a salary or a house but begins with a woman's sense of "belonging" in the place where God has called her. This sense enabled Elisabeth Elliot to make her "home" with her husband's murderers. This sense sent Gladys Aylward across Russia to China, where she had no promise of a place to live. This sense allows Joni Eareckson Tada to pass on a smile from the Lord to her caregiver each morning, even though that smile does not burst forth spontaneously.

This sense of home is what countless Christian women receive from their Savior and offer to others even when they are deprived of affection, food, physical health, friends, educational opportunities, finances, a safe house, or any of the comforts of nice furniture and a fridge full of food. The Christian woman is a homemaker not because she does housework in a habitat constructed for her. She is a "homemaker" because in the power of Christ she creates home wherever she goes. A Christian woman *is* a home.

When Peter and I were students, we spent many Sunday afternoons in the apartment of a young widow whose husband had died after only a few months of marriage. Ginny did not dissolve in grief, but she poured her energies into making a home away from home for college students at Park Street Church. Each Sunday, she made a big pot of chili or stew, a salad, and dessert. After church, students gathered in her apartment to sing, talk, and enjoy one another's company before returning to the evening service. Ginny's willingness to go on making a home even after the tragedy God called her to experience is one reason our home exists. Peter and I became friends in the warmth of her apartment and were forever affected by her courageous hospitality.

All Christian women are called to be homemakers. Your home may be a Starbucks table, where you invite girls from your church to come talk. You may make your home over the telephone, offering encouragement to homebound people. If you are married to an unbeliever, you may have to create home away from home by meeting others at church or in their homes. You may have a huge home that can accommodate a crowd. You may own a camper that provides a home on the road, or have a large backyard where the neighbor children come to play.

Even if you are under such duress that you have no corner to call your own, your enveloping arms offer refuge to another lonely woman, a child, or an elderly person. Adam didn't feel "at home" on earth until Eve arrived!

Just as a woman can make or break the mood of her own home, so the women in a church can make or break the atmosphere in the church. Women who exercise hospitality and carefully watch the mood of their hearts in their own homes will carry those skills into the church. Offering a home in Christ's name, we need the support of other Christians. The unbeliever who experiences the warmth of one Christian home may think he just got lucky to find a family so "nice and hospitable." But when that person meets Christians in a church, where the same hospitality is offered by all, he discovers that the love comes not from the people themselves, but from Christ.

Women have tremendous power in the church. I pray that Christian women will realize the mysterious power they have to make a home from just a house and to exercise that power for the sake of the church, in the name of Christ. A woman happy in her church is more likely to be a happy wife and mother, and a happy wife and mother is likely to be a positive influence for joy in her church. The Christian family and the church family are natural contributors to each other.

Children

One woman told me, "I must be weird, but I've never wanted children." I wonder, though, whether a woman's natural desire for children has been stifled by a moral imperative in our culture to limit children. When I was in college, zero population growth was the ideal. Since then, we have moved from ZPG to NPG—negative population growth. Some groups express the ideal of reducing the world's population by 90 percent!

God is a God of families. He loves marriage and children and commands the first couple to fill the earth. As Christian women, we understand that filling the earth also means bearing "spiritual" children for Christ, but God has not stopped loving physical babies (Isa. 66:7–13). I recently had the privilege of attending the birth of our granddaughter, Miranda. As her mother and father delighted and marveled at their baby daughter, I was, once again, overwhelmed at the privilege and glory of bearing children. The pain of childbirth begins to dissipate the moment a mother catches the eye of her newborn baby, a unique likeness of the Creator.

Some Christian women find it difficult to admit joy in the birth of children because their cultures frown on large families. Some live in countries like China, where the government has declared it illegal to have more than one child. The German woman who wants children must find an affordable apartment big enough to house them. The Christian woman in Sudan is afraid to bear another child because she cannot feed her family on dust, or she doesn't want to see another baby thrown into a fire by vicious bands of thugs.

It sounds idealistic and arrogant for me to advise Christian women to rejoice in having children, but I believe this to be the direction of the Scripture's commands to us: "Behold, children are a heritage from the LORD, the fruit of the womb a reward. Like arrows in the hand of a warrior are the children of one's youth. Blessed is the man who fills his quiver with them! He shall not be put to shame when he speaks with his enemies in the gate" (Ps. 127:3–5 ESV).

Why are we so quick to accept the joys of marriage without accepting one of God's main purposes for it? Certainly, Christian marriage is not for the purpose of reproduction *only*. It represents the rich love of Christ's relationship with the church. But even in that spiritual parallel, the element of growth and reproduction is not absent. The church is a living, growing organism. If it is not growing in wisdom and numbers, growing into the fullness of its head, Jesus Christ, then it can hardly be called the church. Its evangelistic call is clear—to make disciples of every nation. The church cannot truly relate to Christ if it does not enter into Christ's project of filling the universe. New creatures are being born all the time into the household of faith and growing to maturity "in favour with God and man" (Luke 2:52 KJV).

Christian women need to rethink their attitudes toward bearing children. Who says that a law degree is more valuable than a family? Is a trim figure more important than a hug from a trim eighteen-year-old son? Why do we feel it is our job to define the world as already "full"? Surely God will know when the earth is full and when the end of history must come. For the moment, one has only to fly over Arizona to realize that our fears of over-population are somewhat exaggerated. In the meantime, 45,000 people die in an earthquake, AIDS decimates entire generations in Africa, the male sperm count decreases, and the birth rate in some countries has fallen so low that it is mathematically impossible for them to repopulate.

P. D. James wrote a fascinating story called *The Children of Men* in which she imagines a world of barren women, who resort to taking their cats out to the park in baby strollers. If we continue to tell God how many people should live on this planet, we may suffer from a withdrawal of His hand of blessing, as is intimated by Hosea: "They shall play the whore, but not multiply, because they have forsaken the LORD" (Hos. 4:10 ESV). So far, God has continued to bless the human race with children. It is His design and His joy: "He gives the barren woman a home, making her the joyous mother of children. Praise the LORD!" (Ps. 113:9 ESV).

I once witnessed a poignant scene at an airport Starbucks counter. In line, a young, no-rings couple argued heatedly. I couldn't help overhearing what the young man said: "Anyway, you don't deserve to have a baby!" He was not looking at his girlfriend as he said it, but I was. Fierce pain shot across her face and she gasped, then made for the ladies' room, tears brimming from her eyes. I stood for a few seconds, then headed for the restroom myself. I found her and said, "I know I'm a total stranger, but you need a hug. No woman *deserves* a baby, but every woman has the right to long for one. Don't listen to those poisonous words." This young woman's desire for a child was right, though the relationship in which she was involved seemed far from healthy.

Every Sunday one of our church elders prays for women in our church who are hoping to be pregnant. They have scriptural precedent: "May the Lord give you increase, you and your children!" (Ps. 115:14 ESV). We must begin to adapt our thinking to God's, who highly honors and values the bearing and rearing of children. God chose a teenage girl to accomplish a childbearing job on which the existence of the church depended. All of history prepared for the coming of God the King, who burst onto the human scene through the womb of a young woman.

Why do we allow ourselves to fear following God's call to fill the earth? Our salvation, too, as Christian women, hangs on a birth. It remains our privilege and duty to continue in childbearing and in faith. This principle is larger than our individual stories. I am not saying you have to be a mother to be godly. God closes the womb of some women without closing the floodgates of blessing in their lives. What I write here is not meant to make you feel meaningless if God has chosen not to give you children. But if you are ignoring God's call to bear and rear children, then I will not be sorry if my words encourage you to obey.

You may read these words and weep, because you have lost a baby—maybe several babies. You have longed for children and God has said no. You may read these words and weep because, duped by your society, you have aborted your baby. If you are not thinking about babies yet because God hasn't given you a husband, you may wonder why I emphasize the importance of something you may never experience.

My words are not meant to cause anyone pain, but to stimulate hope and courage in the hearts of women who are afraid to have children. Fear can stop some women from becoming mothers—fear of the physical pain of childbirth, fear of losing your figure or not being able to provide for a child, fear that you won't make a good mother. I am sympathetic to those who refuse birth control and are ready to receive the children whom God gives them. But as Christians, we must never fall into moral legalism. There may be times when it is wise to put off having a baby. Personally, I do not believe it is always wrong to control the timing of a baby, as long as a woman is not destroying a baby already conceived. Each couple must pray through such decisions.

But the reasons couples offer are far from biblical: the house is too small, we don't have enough money, the car is not big enough, I might have to quit work. If God gives you a baby, God will take care of your family. The psalmist put it this way, "I have been young and now I am old, yet I have not seen the righteous abandoned or his children begging bread. He is always generous, always lending, and his children are a blessing" (Ps. 37:25–26).

To those of you who have been praying for years for a child, let me say that childlessness is not often a direct punishment for a particular sin.[3] However, the Bible recognizes barrenness as a problem, whereas our culture often sees it as a blessing that allows a woman the chance for a meaningful career. If God has chosen childlessness for you, don't feel surprised or guilty if you still feel a strong desire for children. Even this sadness can be turned to fruitfulness for the King.

The focused ministry of a single woman brings delight to Christ's heart. He received the ministry of such women during His time on earth, and He receives all that you do in His honor. You bring His heart as much joy and delight as any mother. As for advantages, you do not live with the constant temptation to put your children above your Savior, nor do you suffer the anguish of soul that mothers experience as they sometimes must watch their children turn their backs on God's love. If you are childless, you are in wonderful company—the apostle Paul and Jesus, among others, who found their joy in spiritual children.

Today's woman has a hard time believing that true significance can be found at home. What about it? Should motherhood be full-time? Does it preclude doing other valuable things? Can it become an idol?

Can there be a kind of legalism to the "make your own granola and sew the kids' clothes while homeschooling twelve children" mentality?

How do we answer our longing for true significance?

Significance: Marking Eternity

Women mark eternity just as surely as do men. A woman's significance, though linked to her husband's if she is married, is not limited by his significance; nor is it defined by his. A single woman has as much significance as a married woman and can be more single-mindedly devoted to Christ. She reports directly to her heavenly husband and doesn't spend time and money keeping an earthly husband happy. She can eat a yoghurt and an apple for dinner, if she wants, and she can concentrate without interruption on projects of her choice. Even a married woman ultimately looks only to Christ for significance. At the day of judgment she will not face her earthly husband but her heavenly husband.

A woman's longing for significance is good and right. Wanting to make a mark outside our individual homes is also valid. But we must think clearly here. As with all things, the world defines significance differently than God does. As Christians, we want to count in God's eyes. We want His stamp of approval. The four hobbits in *The Return of the King* are stunned when the entire assembly at the white city bows down to them. They can hardly believe that they are the ones honored and celebrated by kings. In our analysis of worth, we must take the wide perspective, seeing the global significance of events. Though the actions of King Aragorn and the wizard Gandalf were crucial to the quest, it was the insignificant hobbits who slipped through enemy lines, faithfully crept to the brink of Mt. Doom, in spite of pain and fatigue, and managed the triumphant act that brought the gates of Mordor crashing down.

Winning the Miss America pageant, making the cover of *Time*, or capturing an Oscar carry their own rewards. Patiently caring for a baby who is sick or cooking your 11,561st meal for your family will not earn you a spot on "Fox and Friends." Like the hobbits, you don't see the significance of your faithfulness—nor do others. But God sees our actions and the desires of our hearts. He does not reward us according to the world's measure, but according to His standard.

God calls women to service which often goes unseen in the world's eyes. When I was visiting my father-in-law some years ago, a delightful and godly retired Latin teacher was visiting, along with her elderly mother. After tea, Ruth helped her mother prepare to leave, taking painstaking minutes to help her put on white gloves, a hat, and a coat. Then they walked to the door. "Walked" is an exaggeration. Ruth's mother could only shuffle forward at the pace of about a foot a minute. I would never have had the patience to walk quietly beside this genteel saint of God. I would have said, "OK, Mom. Let's go!" and swept her up in my arms, or popped her into a wheelchair.

Were the ten minutes it took them to cross the room wasted moments in Ruth's life? Never! Every step will one day be sung about by the angels. It is the Ruths of this world who are most likely to be at the head of the parade in heaven. God's values are not ours. Every shuffle Ruth's mother made was a step toward heaven, not only for the older woman, but for Ruth and, in a sense, for all of us.

Such honor is not unseen in God's eyes and it does not go unnoticed in the eyes of the heavenly powers. In explaining how the gospel now reaches to the ends of the world, Paul says: "This is so that God's multi-faceted wisdom may now be made known through the church to the rulers and authorities in the heavens" (Eph. 3:10). He then encourages the Ephesian believers not to be discouraged about his imprisonment. Throughout the book of Ephesians this theme comes through. God's church—in its weakness and suffering, in its imprisonments, in the moments when no one is watching, in the details of changing diapers or scrubbing floors—is the agent of God's power and wisdom in the world. The evil powers are watching, attempting to draw God's saints away from their primary purpose of serving and loving God.

The calling God has placed on women serves the gospel in power. When you are alone with your child and you fight off the temptation to shake your little one in frustration, you have won a mighty battle in the kingdom. The evil powers in the heavenlies are watching. You have shown them God's wisdom and power. You have torn down another brick from the gates of hell.

What significance are we seeking as women? Why do we accept the world's standards of significance? Are we so blind as to think that the trappings of glory offered to us if we break the glass ceiling outshine the glory the angels will sing of us when we stand by the sea of glass in the golden city before the throne of our King, our Savior, our Husband?

Our God has asked us to fulfill a job. It may seem small and insignificant. It may seem humiliating and second class. But God has defined what He wants us to do. He has given us the gifts, the power, and the love necessary for our task, and He promises to establish the work of our hands. Has He not made us women? Do we not owe it to Him to follow His design for our lives, rather than seeking our honor from the lips of the world?

Conclusion

All the desires of a woman's heart are met in service of Christ: good relationships with men and with other women; a true home; children, both physical and spiritual; and eternal significance. Feminism's challenge has caused Christians to think through the women's issue and to understand the richness and beauty of God's clear and unchanging design for women, from the first days of creation to the first years of our twenty-first century. Christian women not only find personal satisfaction in this design, but they have the honor of showing the gospel to the world in their daily lives.

How Christians think about and live out our male-female distinctions is one of the foremost evangelistic tools in reaching those who have not understood the gospel. The "women's issue" is not secondary, but central to the proclamation of the gospel in the twenty-first century.

■　■　■

Discussion Questions

1. How does a Christian woman live differently?

2. Which of your daily activities go unnoticed? To whom are you showing the gospel in these tasks?

3. What activities of value to our society may not be so impressive to God?

4. In what ways has your idea of womanhood been defined by your upbringing? Your education? The media? The Bible?

5. In which of the five areas we've mentioned (relationships with men, with women, rearing children, having a home, and having significance) do you feel the least fulfilled? The most? Are these areas equal over the span of your life as a woman?

6. Has your perspective on these areas changed over your lifetime? In what way?

7. Should it change the way you do dishes to know that you are showing the wisdom of God to the "heavenly powers"? (see Eph. 3:10).

8. What are your most precious woman-to-woman relationships? How could you help encourage such relationships in your church?

9. As a woman, how can you encourage the men with whom you have contact?

10. What is your "home"? How does it differ from that of other women? How can you use your home as a safe haven for those who need some mothering?

■ ■ ■

Resources

Elliot, Elisabeth. *Let Me Be a Woman.* Carol Stream, Ill.: Tyndale, 1999.

Fitzpatrick, Elyse and Carol Cornish. *Women Helping Women.* Eugene, Ore.: Harvest House, 1997.

Henry, Barbara. *Woman to Woman: Life Principles from Titus 2.* Chattanooga, Tenn.: AMG, 2003.

Hunt, Susan and Peggy Hutcheson. *Leadership for Women in the Church.* Grand Rapids: Zondervan, 1991.

Hunt, Susan. *The True Woman: The Beauty and Strength of a Godly Woman.* Wheaton, Ill.: Crossway, 1997.

Kelley, Rhonda H. *Communication between Men and Women in the Context of the Christian Community.* Booklet, available at www.cbmw.org.

Kennedy, Nancy. *When He Doesn't Believe: Help and Encouragement for Women Who Feel Alone in Their Faith.* New York: Waterbrook Press, 2001.

Macauley, Susan. *For the Family's Sake: The Value of Home in Everyone's Life.* Wheaton, Ill.: Crossway, 1999.

Morley, Donna. *A Woman of Significance.* Wheaton, Ill.: Crossway, 2001.

Strauch, Alexander. *Hospitality Commands.* Lewis and Roth, 1993.

If I profess with the loudest voice and clearest exposition every portion of the truth of God except precisely that little point which the world and the devil are at that moment attacking, I am not confessing Christ, however boldly I may be professing Christ. Where the battle rages, there the loyalty of the soldier is proved; and to be steady on all the battlefield besides, is mere flight and disgrace if he flinches at that point.

—MARTIN LUTHER

12

Why It Matters

IN 2000, THE Southern Baptist Convention changed its "Baptist Faith and Message" for the first time since 1963. Here is part of its statement on the family:

> The husband and wife are of equal worth before God, since both are created in God's image. The marriage relationship models the way God relates to His people. A husband is to love his wife as Christ loved the church. He has the God-given responsibility to provide for, to protect, and to lead his family. A wife is to submit herself graciously to the servant leadership of her husband even as the church willingly submits to the headship of Christ. She, being in the image of God as is her husband and thus equal to him, has the God-given responsibility to respect her husband and to serve as his helper in managing the household and nurturing the next generation.[1]

This change set off a furor within the denomination and in the press. But the Baptists are not playing politics or clinging to a June Cleaver social ideal; they have the apostle Paul behind them. Women who refuse God's design bring scandal on the gospel: "Older women are to be reverent in behavior, not slanderers, not addicted to much wine. They are to teach what is good, so that they may encourage the young women to love their husbands and children, to be sensible, pure, good homemakers, and submissive to their husbands, *so that God's message will not be slandered*" (Titus 2:3–5, emphasis added).

In another passage, Paul reiterates his warning: "I want younger women to marry, have children, manage their households, and *give the adversary no opportunity to accuse us*" (1 Tim. 5:14, emphasis added).

Today, it seems that holding to the biblical teaching about marriage, the family, and the place of the woman is exactly what *does* "give the adversary an opportunity to accuse us." Many Christians, even godly pastors, feel the "women's issue" is secondary and that the peace and witness of the church should not be disturbed for a peripheral issue. But Paul ties our sexual identity inextricably to the gospel message because an attack on sexual structures is an attack on God's authority over creation. The marriage structure was woven into the fabric of creation to teach us of God's nature as Creator, to show us the intimacy and communion of the Trinity, and to picture for us God's faithful love for His people. Marriage is a still-life that reflects a deeper life of union with Him.

The picture reflects an infinite reality. When we mess with it, we distort how God is seen and understood. Paul shows us that a refusal to glorify God as Creator leads inevitably to the disintegration of normal sexual relationships (Rom. 1:18–25). Christians cannot afford to abandon God's design for marriage and for sexual differentiation. Our dedication to marriage professes our confident faith in the Creator and offers a living portrait of the gospel to those wandering through the cobwebs of bogus spirituality and counterfeit sexuality.

The attack on heterosexual fidelity is an attack on God, who put distinctions in our world. Man is not to put asunder what God has united, but neither is man to unite what God has put asunder. Men and women are *not* the same, but they were set apart to serve distinct created functions still valid in service to Christ. The Holy Spirit who breathed out God's creation also gives us resurrection power to infuse God's created structures with love, joy, and light. We who stand on this side of the resurrection of Jesus Christ have a better understanding of marriage than Adam and Eve. We are united in indissoluble bonds of love to the heavenly Bridegroom, who is the first new man, the progenitor of a new race.

It is Christ's bride who bears holy offspring to God. We, the church, are responsible for bearing physical children set apart for God's service, and for bearing spiritual children, adopted into God's family in love. As we live the distinctions of our sexual makeup and the distinctions of our calling as God's children, we declare to the world that God has authority over us and that He is not to be confused with His creation. Our culture has decided to redirect the earth, forming it after its own designs and trying to become absorbed by the earth itself as an expression of spirituality. We cannot allow human beings to be swallowed up by the earth—to lose their identity as uniquely "image of God." Our world has gone wild, mixing genetic material from distinct races, spilling precious human seed on the ground by discarding semen and even tiny human babies in the trash, blurring the distinctions between man and animal, and redefining human sexuality according to its perverted whims.

Those who wish to destroy the sexual distinctions will attempt to show that Christians are narrow in their thinking, and even "haters of humanity," as they were called in the first century (though it was Christians who rescued and adopted abandoned babies). The conflict between those who love God's creational distinctions and those who hate them is of the deepest nature. There is no possibility of believing at the same time that there *are no* distinctions and that there *are* distinctions. Christians who hold to God's distinctions will one day face persecution for their stance. Already in Canada pastors are feeling the pressure to remain silent in their pulpits about the Bible's teachings on homosexuality. If they teach clearly what God has revealed, they may contravene laws against "hate speech" and be sanctioned with two years in prison.

Christians have the challenging but glorious opportunity not only to defend creational structures logically and scripturally, but to embody God's creational idea. As we affirm the male-female distinctions and live out a "one man-one woman for life" marriage in the context of the church, Christ's bride, we embody God's glory to the world. Our marriages and our church relationships show the world what unity with Christ means. We embody God's creational structures when we willingly bear children and teach them of the love of their Savior. We embody God's creational structures as we live morally and in harmony with the earth, exercising our authority over it, guarding it, keeping it, loving it, but not worshipping it.

God the Creator who "sits above the circle of the earth" (Isa. 40:22 ESV) condescended to enter our world as a baby, Jesus, born of a woman. Christians who are united to God through the work of Christ stand on a rock that cannot be shaken, even when the rocks of earth come crashing down around us. We have a word, the Word, which sets us free because it is the truth. We are commanded to share that truth with those around us, whether they want to listen or not. Affirming the male-female distinction is a crucial aspect of declaring God's truth in today's world.

Speaking of God's distinctions is one thing. We must also show that truth in our bodies. As we hold firm to the sexuality that God has given us and defined for us, we will have an effect on the earth, slowing moral decay and showing how tasty life really is. One day the purpose of human marriage will be fulfilled. Women and men, still unique in God's image, will know relationships with each other and with God that will so surpass the beauty of marriage that the highest ecstasies and the deepest intimacies of human marriage will appear as the embarrassed stammerings of puppy love.

I speak to myself as well as to the women reading this book. May we rejoice in our femininity, defining it not as the world does, but as Christ does. Let's honor our husbands, actively submitting to them and seeking to bring all that is in our realm of authority under their headship, until that glorious day when they will lay all at the feet of Christ, who will, in turn, lay all at the feet of His Father. As Christian women in our churches, we must not wrest authority out of the hands of its God-declared leaders, but rather seek their heart for gospel witness and align our energies behind them. We women can delight in showing the world that God made women glorious, in His image, not to be squashed but to work for His honor in our homes, churches, and society with grace, power, and eloquence. We do not attempt such obedience in our own strength, but beg God's Spirit to fill us with power and joy. "He who started a good work in you will carry it on to completion until the day of Christ Jesus" (Phil. 1:6). God will establish the work of our hands. In serving Him as women, we will find true satisfaction and make our mark on the world and on eternity.

As Christ beautifies us in His image may we, with all those who are a part of His body, His bride, speak out for Him in this world of despair, and by His Spirit say by our actions, words, and spirit as Christian women to all we meet, "Come! Come join us at the wedding feast of our bridegroom, Jesus!"

■   ■   ■

Discussion Questions

1. Does the "feminism" issue seem secondary or of first importance to you in society? In the church? Why or why not?

2. In what way has this book changed your thinking about being a woman?

3. How can you affirm your feminine, created nature in your everyday life? In your family? In your workplace? In your relationship with God?

4. How would you defend Christian marriage? In light of the distinctions put in the world at creation, what do you think of gay marriage? How should a Christian relate to this issue politically?

5. If you have felt squashed as a woman, where have these feelings come from—your own rebellion against God's design for you as a woman, or objective mistreatment? What should you do about the former? About the latter?

6. Has this book changed your thinking in any way about your marriage? About your body? About having children? If so, in what ways?

7. What would you say is your greatest discouragement or point of resistance to God's design for your life as a woman? How can the gospel help you in this area?

8. How can you as a woman encourage the men in your life? How would you encourage men who are not Christians?

9. What can you do in your church, your home, your school, or your community to help people understand why God made men and women to be different?

10. Why is it "blasphemous" for a woman not to please God in her actions as a woman? (see 1 Tim. 6:1; Titus 3:2).

■ ■ ■

Resources

Carson, D. A. *The Gagging of God*. Grand Rapids: Zondervan, 2002.

Grudem, Wayne. *Why Human Sexuality Is at the Center of Many Current Controversies*. Two-page chart, available at www.cbmw.org.

Heimbach, Daniel R. *True Moral Sexuality: Recovering Biblical Standards for a Culture in Crisis.* Wheaton, Ill.: Crossway, 2004.

Jones, Peter R. *Capturing the Pagan Mind: Paul's Blueprint for Thinking and Living in the New Global Culture.* Nashville: Broadman & Holman, 2003.

————. *Biblical Manhood & Womanhood and the Contemporary Collapse of Sexual Morals.* Booklet, available at www.cbmw.org.

————. *Gospel Truth, Pagan Lies: Can You Tell the Difference?* Escondido, Calif.: Main Entry Editions, 2000, reprint 2004.

————. *The Gnostic Empire Strikes Back: An Old Heresy for the New Age.* Phillipsburg, N.J.: P&R, 1992.

————. Androgyny: "The Pagan Sexual Ideal," *Journal of the Evangelical Theological Society,* September 2000. Can be read at www.cwipp.org (www.spirit-wars.com/v25/english/Library/Articles/Androgyny.htm).

Patterson, Dorothy. *The Family: Unchanging Principles for Changing Times.* Nashville: Broadman & Holman, 2002.

Sears, Alan, and Craig Osten. *The Homosexual Agenda: Exposing the Principal Threat to Religious Freedom Today.* Nashville: Broadman & Holman, 2003.

Veith, Gene Edwards. *Postmodern Times: A Christian Guide to Contemporary Thought and Culture.* Wheaton, Ill.: Crossway, 1994.

Welch, Ed. *Homosexuality: Speaking the Truth in Love.* Phillipsburg, N.J.: 2000.

www.cwipp.org

Yungen, Ray. *A Time of Departing: How a Universal Spirituality Is Changing the Face of Christianity.* Silverton, Ore.: Lighthouse Trails Publishing Company, 2002.

Notes

Chapter One

Epigraphs. First: www.zonezero.com/exposiciones/fotografos/
girlcult/Greenfield 18.html#. Second: See Lauren Greenfield's photographic essay, "Girl Culture," www.dizzy.library.arizona.edu/
branches/ccp/education/girlculturefacultyguide/index.html.

1. See Marilyn Ferguson, "Aquarius Now . . . Making It through the
Confusion Gap," *Visions Magazine* (July 1994): 7.

2. *National Review* (16 June 2003): 6.

3. Gene Edward Veith, "Identity Crisis," *World Magazine* (27 March
2004): 27.

4. Susan Jacoby, "Atrocity Knows No Gender," *Los Angeles Times*
(11 May 2004), B15.

5. For a sampling of articles on these issues, see www.realm-of-
shade.com/meretrix/links/ general.shtml.

6. See www.news.wisc.edu/view.html?get=6069.

7. Kate Millet, *Sexual Politics* (Garden City, New York: Doubleday,
1970), 250f.

8. For example, the Earth Charter and Agenda 21. You can read the
Earth Charter from the following Web site: www.earthcharterusa
.org/earth_charter.html. See also www.populationconnection.org/
Communications/FactSheets/WomensEmpowerment.pdf. For Agenda
21, see www.un.org/esa/sustdev/documents/agenda21/index.htm.

9. Take, for example, the "Population Connection" statement: "At
root, population issues are quality-of-life issues. History shows us that
as population growth slows in a country, the quality of life in that country rises. We advocate for population stabilization as an essential step in
ensuring a high quality of life for everyone." See www.population
connection.org/ kidfriendlycountries/ Pages/why.htm.

10. www.motherjones.com/news/feature/1995/09/women.mali.html.

11. See the United Nations document A/CONF.151/26 (vol. 1) Rio Statement Principle 8: "To achieve sustainable development and a higher quality of life for all people, States should reduce and eliminate unsustainable patterns of production and consumption and promote appropriate demographic policies." www.un.org/documents/ga/conf151/aconf15126-1annex1.htm. Consult, also, the documents produced at the Fourth World Conference on Women, in Beijing, China (1995).

12. Some working mothers are beginning to take at least a few years out to look after their children. See *The Case for Staying Home, Time Magazine* (22 March 2004): 51–59.

13. I did read this in an interview with Bright but wouldn't recommend the Web site, which contains much offensive material.

14. Greenfield, *Girl Culture.*

15. Idem.

16. www.reimagining.org/smallgrp.html. See Minnesota, St. Paul entry.

17. Marjorie Coeyman, "What Women Want—To Read" (www.csmonitor.com/ 2002/0606/p11s03-ussc.html).

18. Danielle Crittenden, *What Our Mothers Didn't Tell Us* (New York: Simon and Schuster, 1999), 13.

19. Virginia Mollenkott, *Sensual Spirituality: Out from Fundamentalism* (New York: Crossroads, 1992), 73.

20. Andrew Greeley, *Omni Magazine* (January 1987): 98.

21. Naomi Goldenberg, cited in Mary A. Kassian, *The Feminist Gospel: The Movement to Unite Feminism with the Church* (Wheaton, Ill.: Crossway Books, 1992), 220.

Chapter Two

1. I speak at length about the marriage relationship because it is the norm for male-female interaction, and for other reasons that will become evident. Single readers will understand parallels in their own lives, in which the principles of this book are still applicable, though they will be worked out differently.

2. Dorothy Sayers and Jill Paton Walsh, *Thrones, Dominations* (New York: St. Martin's Press, 1998).

3. The Bible uses such imagery to talk about God so that we can understand something of Him. Of course, saying that God writes something with His "finger" does not mean He has a human body.

4. Alice Walker, *The Color Purple* (New York: Simon and Schuster, 1982), 203.

Chapter Three

1. C. S. Lewis, *The Silver Chair* (New York: Macmillan, 1953), 155.

2. Something "androgynous" means a blending of male and female, and comes from the Greek words *andros* and *gynos* (man and woman). Another word with the same meaning is "gynandrous."

3. See also the more cited passage, "Let Us make man in Our image, according to Our likeness," says the triune God. "So God created man in His own image; He created him in the image of God; He created them male and female" (Gen. 1:26–27).

4. First Corinthians 15:22: "For just as in Adam all die, so also in Christ all will be made alive"; Hos. 6:7: "But they, like Adam, have violated the covenant; there they have betrayed Me."

5. This is the apostle Paul's argument. See 1 Tim. 2:11–14.

6. Romans 5:14: "Nevertheless, death reigned from Adam to Moses, even over those who did not sin in the likeness of Adam's transgression. He is a prototype of the Coming One." (Notice that Adam is cited, not Eve.)

7. The television production "The Rise of Evil" depicts those around Hitler who allowed him power even though it made them despair.

8. Henry Law, *All Is Christ: The Gospel in Genesis* (1854: reprint, Edinburgh: Banner of Truth Trust, 1993), 48, speaking of the animals who died to clothe Adam and Eve, says: "They were offered in sacrifice. Thus they foreshadowed the Lamb 'foreordained before the foundation of the world.' And hence we learn that in Eden victims bled. Yes! the first drop, which stained the earth, the first expiring groan, proclaimed in the most intelligible terms, 'the wages of sin is death'; and 'without shedding of blood is no remission.' The doctrine of these rites is the doctrine of the Cross."

9. The same phrase used in Genesis 3:16 appears in Genesis 4:7, where God exhorts Cain: "Sin is crouching at the door. Its desire is for you, but you must master it."

10. See Acts 17:28.

11. Micah says this to God's people, who were sacrificing their children to idols. Humans cannot thus buy their way into God's presence. God Himself must provide the sacrifice.

Chapter Four

1. Vashti refused to obey King Ahasuerus and was relieved of her crown. Esther was obedient to the king, thus gaining his favor and enabling her to later plead the cause of the Jewish people in his kingdom.

2. I calculated Old Testament sermons by examining online sermons from ten Web sites of my own denomination, known for its commitment to seeing Christ in all the Scripture. Only 11 percent were preached from the Old Testament (including one Old Testament series, whose percentage was therefore 100 percent). Forty percent had no Old Testament text listed.

3. See, for example, David J. A. Clines, *Interested Parties: The Ideology of Writers and Readers of the Hebrew Bible* (*Journal for the Study of the Old Testament Supplement Series,* 205; *Gender Culture, Theory,* 1; Sheffield: Sheffield Academic Press, 1995), 187–211.

4. Miriam Therese Winter, *The Chronicles of Noah and Her Sisters: Genesis and Exodus According to Women* (New York: Crossroad, Herter and Herter, 1995).

5. *The Five Gospels: What Did Jesus Really Say? The Search for the AUTHENTIC Words of Jesus* by Robert Funk (HarperSanFrancisco, 1997).

6. For help in understanding this threat, see James Garlow and Peter Jones, *Cracking Da Vinci's Code* (Colorado Springs, Colo.: Victor Books, 2004).

7. See Peter Jones, *Spirit Wars: Pagan Revival in Christian America* (Mukilteo, Wash.: Main Entry Editions and Winepress Publishing, 1997), 122.

8. God mercifully does not reject us when we misuse His Word, if we have a heart of faith. Instead, He leads us gently to a deeper understanding. Those with a deeper understanding of the Bible must be gracious as they encourage others to discover its richness.

9. I chose only one element of this passage as an example for Bible interpretation.

10. The *urim* and *thummim* was a "yes/no" system (perhaps white and black stones) the priest used to reveal God's will. David consulted it, for example, to see if he should go to battle.

Chapter Five

1. In the movie, these are Aragorn's words to a boy warrior frightened on the eve of battle.

2. "Patriarchy" (the rule of the father) can be a powerful good if it means the loving leadership of godly men according to creation structures.

3. The tragic fate of Cain surely devastated Eve. Far from rescuing the new race, he murdered his only brother.

4. God protects the identity of Sarah's child by rendering all women in Abimelech's kingdom sterile. If no children were being conceived, Sarah's pregnancy could not have begun in Abimelech's land.

5. Othniel and Ehud are "raised up" by God as "saviors" or "deliverers." Shamgar "saved" Israel. Deborah, a "judge," has God's blessing as she rouses fearful men like Barak. The Spirit of the Lord "fell" on Gideon and Samson, both announced by the angel of the Lord, but they were not faithful to God's laws. Abimelech is an evil man on whom falls a "spirit of evil." He is made king by evil men. Tola "defended" Israel but was not "raised up" by the Spirit of God. Jair simply "judged" Israel twenty years. Though Jephthah was elected, he confirmed the oath he made to the Gileadites before the Lord, and the Spirit of the Lord "fell on him."

6. Shamgar's only recorded act was killing six hundred Philistines with an ox goad. Samson could not have doled out much wisdom under Deborah's palm tree. Deborah administered justice but had no calling to war, whereas war was Othniel's chief duty (Judg. 3:10 NIV).

7. Isaiah's wife is called a "prophetess" (Isa. 8:3)

8. See Easton's Bible Dictionary, entry 401: "Baal-Tamar, lord of palm trees, a place in the tribe of Benjamin near Gibeah of Saul" (Judg. 20:33). It was one of the sanctuaries or groves of Baal. Probably the palm tree of Deborah. Judges 4:5 is alluded to in the name.

9. Moses' father-in-law, a Kenite, gave Moses sound advice in administering justice. Later, the Kenites followed the clan of Judah and settled in their territories. Jael's family, however, as we are told in Judges 4:11, had gone off on its own to the north and settled near the Sea of Galilee.

10. See Deuteronomy 17:14–20. The king is not to have multiple wives, and is to be: chosen by God from his fellow Israelites; disinterested in wealth; unwilling to depend on Egypt for help; taken up with the law of the Lord on which he meditates day and night; and careful to follow every law exactly and perfectly.

11. Second Chronicles 19:4–8 (ESV): "Jehoshaphat . . . appointed judges in the land in all the fortified cities of Judah, city by city, and said to the judges, 'Consider what you do, for you judge not for man but for the LORD. He is with you in giving judgment . . .' Moreover, in Jerusalem Jehoshaphat appointed certain Levites and priests and

heads of families of Israel, to give judgment for the LORD and to decide disputed cases. They had their seat at Jerusalem."

Perhaps in the troubled times of the judges, Deborah had been appointed by the Levites to her position of judge, for lack of any wise
male leaders. (Given the infidelity of the Levites in Judges, this seems
doubtful. The priests and Levites mentioned in the book are woe-
fully corrupt.) The Lord's word to Moses tells the Israelites to obey
the judges placed over them by the priests: "If cases come before your
courts that are too difficult for you to judge—whether bloodshed,
lawsuits or assaults—take them to the place the LORD your God will
choose. Go to the priests, who are Levites, and to the judge who is in
office at that time. Inquire of them and they will give you the verdict"
(Deut. 17:8–9 NIV). However, even if Deborah was put in place by the
Levites, we cannot use such a practice as a direct example to follow.
Not much in the book of Judges serves us as an ideal arrangement to
be applied to church life today.

12. The Hebrew name for a Calebite sounds like the word for dog,
leading to a common slur on Calebites that called them "dogs."
Calebites shared ancestry with the tribe of Judah, but caused some
friction over land rights, going back to the time of Joshua, when Caleb
inherited the town of Hebron and its surrounding villages.

13. See Harold Kallemeyn, "Folie, violence et vengeance en
1 Samuel 24 a 26." *La Revue Réformée.* 224. 2003/4, Septembre 2003
Tome LIII, 1ff.

Chapter Six

1. Joseph is willing to sacrifice his reputation for the sake of his purity. Judah, on the other hand, is willing to sacrifice his reputation for
the sake of his lust.

2. Abigail, Rebecca, the woman of Tekoah, and Esther come to
mind. David, Moses, and Paul also express similar feelings.

3. Ronald Bergey offers interesting reflections on God's justice toward the pagan nations in Joshua's time: "La conquête de Canaan: un
génocide?" *La Revue Réformée.* 225. 2003/5, Novembre 2003. Tome
LIV, 69ff.

4. This verse implies that there may have been some choice available
to other inhabitants of Jericho to surrender to the Israelites and to
show their obedience to the God whom Rahab recognized.

5. Because biblical genealogies sometimes skip generations, Boaz
may not be the son of Rahab, but her descendant.

Chapter Seven

Epigraph: J. Gresham Machen, *The Virgin Birth of Christ* (Ann Arbor, Mich.: Baker, 1965), 395.

1. Scholars do not agree on the identity of Mary's family members, but we do know she had a sister. See John 19:25.

2. See Peter Jones, *Spirit Wars: Pagan Revival in Christian America* (Mukilteo, Wash.: Winepress, 1997), 166.

3. Some scholars think the genealogy of Luke is that of Mary, but the point is valid even if only one family line runs through Joseph.

4. Jeconiah's name was shortened to "Coniah," taking out the syllable of God's name. God puts a curse on his descendants: "Write this man down as childless, a man who shall not succeed in his days, for none of his offspring shall succeed in sitting on the throne of David and ruling again in Judah" (Jer. 22:30 ESV).

Chapter Eight

1. This statement, made in the context of a society in which only the male could initiate divorce, does not mean that a woman is never at fault in provoking divorce.

2. He *may* have slept outdoors. Luke 21:37 says, "During the day, He was teaching in the temple complex, but in the evening He would go out and spend the night on what is called the Mount of Olives."

3. The high priest says to Jesus, "Tell us if you are the Christ" (Matt. 26:63 ESV); the chief priests tell Jesus to come down from the cross to prove He is the Christ (Mark 15:32); Simeon states his belief (Luke 2:30); the demons cry, "You are the Son of God" (Luke 4:41); Andrew brings Peter to Jesus with the words, "We have found the Messiah!" (John 1:41); people from Jerusalem say, "Can it be that the authorities really know that this is the Christ?" (John 7:26 ESV); some admit that Jesus is the Christ; others said, "This is the Messiah" (John 7:40).

4. See Luke 8:2. The Greek makes it clear that those serving were women.

Chapter Nine

Epigraph: Geoffrey W. Bromiley, *God and Marriage* (Eugene, Ore.: Wipf and Stock, 1980), 77.

1. www.cryonet.org/cgi-bin/dsp.cgi?msg=22341.

2. I use the words *bride* and *church* interchangeably. *The church* is not a building, a particular national group, a political structure, or a

religious institution. It is personal and organic, the body of believers that stretches across geographical and temporal boundaries. It is all those who will live forever, united to Christ, when this world's history is over.

3. God's Word calls us to engage our wills in following our Lord. Joshua calls out to the Israelites, "Choose this day whom you will serve" (Josh. 24:15). However, we can easily slip into the mistake of thinking that we have all the deciding power and that God is under our control.

Chapter Ten

Epigraph: www.lyrics007.com/Bette%20Midler%20Lyrics/Rose's %20Turn%20Lyrics.html.

1. Ibid.

2. Kate Millett, quoted in Peter Jones, *Spirit Wars: Pagan Revival in Christian America* (Winepress & Main Entry Editions, Mukilteo, Wash.: 1997), 179.

3. The link is grammatically underlined by a shared, unrepeated verb in verses 21 and 22: "submitting one to another . . . wives to your husbands." For a thorough discussion, see Wayne Grudem, "The Myth of Mutual Submission as an Interpretation of Ephesians 5:21," *Biblical Foundations for Manhood and Womanhood,* ed. Wayne Grudem (Wheaton, Ill.: Crossway Books, 2002), 221–232.

4. When we arrive at this stage, we are still in passive mode. It is not, of course, "neutral" to be filled with the Holy Spirit, whose presence leads us to active obedience.

5. The NIV translation reflects the root of the verb which includes the notion of "head." Paul often connects the notion of "fullness" with the notion of headship. See Colossians 1:18–19; 2:10; Ephesians 1:22–23; 2:20 and 3:19 (following his argument "for this reason"); 4:10, 12, 15.

6. Read Ephesians to see how the church is conformed to her husband's plans. She receives much (constructions are passive: be filled, be strengthened, be built up, etc.), but the grace overflows in active service (expose darkness, live a life of love, be imitators of God, etc.).

7. The answer to the first question in the Westminster Catechism for children: "What is man's chief end?"

8. First Corinthians 11:7–10. This reference to angels is the subject of much debate. It is surely related to God's presence with His people. In the Old Testament, two cherubim guarded the ark of the covenant,

the symbol of God's presence. They protected God's people from His holiness which destroys sinners. This structure changes in the New Testament, since at Christ's death God tears the curtain that veiled the Holy of Holies, and His holiness breaks out on Christ, judging sin. The presence of God in the Holy Spirit is now on the move, bringing God's glory to the ends of the earth. Nonetheless, God's gathered people still take seriously the holiness of His presence among them. The last we see of the cherubim in the Old Testament, they are hovering over the East Gate of Jerusalem, the people's access to the temple. That gate, which was to be shut except on the Sabbath day, remains forever open when Christ finalizes his salvation (Rev. 21:23–25) in the city to come. In 1 Corinthians 11, Paul gives instructions about the church's worship while in the already/not yet stage. God's glory is placed on the man, on the woman, on the gathered people, and on Christ. In recognition of God's design, the woman recognizes the authority under which God has placed her and is thus covered with glory. She comes to the God of glory in worship and in prayer, covered by the protective cloud of glory that Christ provides by His death, but also by the protective glory of her husband's authority, provided for her by God's created structure of marriage. She is safe under the covering of Christ, and under the secondary covering of her husband. To accept such a God-ordained place is also her witness before the angels of her recognition of God's holy authority.

Chapter Eleven

Epigraph: Cited by Albert Mohler, "A Call for Courage on Biblical Manhood and Womanhood," www.cbmw.org/news/ram161203.php.

1. The church has an urgent responsibility to protect women, but Yvette's desire to stay with her husband was not necessarily "codependence." Women are not stupid enough to desire suffering! Some, however, have a measure of faith that affords them peace in very difficult situations. Peter teaches that God honors their suffering, which is not the worst thing for a Christian (1 Pet. 2:19), though it is to be avoided if possible. Great wisdom is needed to discern God's will in each situation. One independent church sent its elders to beat up any man found abusing his wife!

2. Some Christian women may, of course, be tempted to lesbianism, especially in a society that is so confused about sexuality. Church women's groups need to know the signs of an unhealthy relationship. I recommend the resources offered by John and Penny Freeman of Harvest USA in Philadelphia.

3. God did take David and Bathsheba's son because of David's sin (see 2 Sam. 12).

Chapter Twelve

Epigraph: Martin Luther, *Weimar Ausgabe Briefwechsel* 3, 81f.
1. www.sbc.net/bfm/bfm2000.asp#xviii.